TRANSANYTHING

TRANSANYTHING

ESSAYS

EVER JONES

CURBSTONE BOOKS / NORTHWESTERN UNIVERSITY PRESS
EVANSTON, ILLINOIS

Curbstone Books
Northwestern University Press
www.nupress.northwestern.edu

Printed in the United States of America

10 9 8 7 6 5 4 3 2 1

ISBN 978-0-8101-4870-3 (paper)
ISBN 978-0-8101-4871-0 (ebook)

Cataloging-in-Publication Data are available from the Library of Congress.

for Corinne and my family

I cannot write a “whole” book about a broken world.

—Mab Segrest, *Born to Belonging*

CONTENTS

PREFACE

Preface: Staring at it, you might picture a face before its features. A pre-face: The moment before you begin to memorize the way a person's eyes arrest their face or the particular harmony of cheekbone and jaw. You might picture the ghostly moment when the portrait painter outlines the face then smudges it with skin color; smudges it into an approximation haunted like a feverish apparition—not a far cry from the historylessness imposed by a colonial empire intent upon controlling the narrative.

There is something to be said about taking in a person's face—to really look. It feels like falling in love every time, the connection of looking, the openness to study their history, their way of inhabiting a moment, to really face it. Not a pre-face, but a turn and face.

In generative somatic therapy, one cornerstone of the practice is blending: learning to blend with your trauma and conflict, to face it, rather than avoiding or fighting against it. The first step is to identify a past or a present conflict and talk it through. Then stand across the room from your therapist, them signifying the issue, you breathing and centering, becoming present in your body, preparing to blend with it—preparing to face it. In this embodied practice, walk up to the therapist—your issue—repeatedly, turning and facing, turning and facing until you make an embodied connection. The process can take months or years. This is the process of unraveling a knot.

How often do we allow ourselves to really face another person or to face our wounds? What would our world look like if we opened wound to wound—that particular harmony? Staring at it. Would we feel less lonely?

As a trans and nonbinary person, when I think of being seen I contract into a twisted puzzle of myself, in *the stance of someone just departed*, a phrase I borrow from Rilke, which, if you google it, leads to advertisements for psychic mediums. I see the connection. When I imagine the phrase, I see its contradiction: How can someone have just departed yet still embody a stance? Whether the spirit leaves the body because of death or as a coping mechanism for survival, I suppose there is still the body—its position and configuration. I think of it as a walking away from while still looking.

When I was little and my mom would try to get me to wear a dress, I'd feel an incredible loneliness. When my paternal grandma would make comments about me being a girl, I shrank. When I joined the Girl Scouts hoping to make cool knots and build fires but was given string to crochet, I left my body then left the meeting. I biked around the neighborhood with my BMX biking pads until I was sure the meeting was over, then headed home. All I told my mom was that I didn't like it. I was six years old.

What is truer is that I was not being seen. It was the 1970s and I was assigned female at birth and from that moment the heteronormative gaze pinned all kinds of meanings to me: dresses, Barbies, dolls, playing house, liking boys—even passivity. And when a meaning didn't fit, I was *other*, and always *just departed.* On my kindergarten report card it said, "X is a wonderful student but doesn't seem to like playing with others." Except I did want to play. But I was asked to make pretend and play house, and I couldn't imagine getting that right.

It took me over forty years to face myself. To turn and face, day after day, the complex equation I had become. When I finally imagined myself without breasts, when I hypothetically injected testosterone and imagined losing my curves, I could take a picture of myself; I could paint my portrait. It is a portrait built upon change, wound to wound, a feeling into. It is a way of looking that resists the loneliness I'd learned to inhabit.

Now, I sometimes look at people this way—this full fathom—and I wonder if having a coffee or beer with me sometimes feels like being on a date. Connection is not romantic, nor is it reserved for partners and spouses—but it is an intimacy, a rare one rendered taboo in a settler colonial society rooted in individualism, determined in monogamy. But facing it is patient, soft, unreserved, every identity and no identity simultaneously; it is made of change, is spirit-like; it is undetermined and pedagogical—like feeling your way into a portrait rather than capturing the subject. It is possible if you transanything.

Céline Sciamma's film *Portrait of a Lady on Fire* is a revelation in looking. The first words of the movie include *take time to look at me* and the final words are *turn around.* Set in late-1800s France, the film documents the relationship between Marianne, a portrait artist, and the aristocrat Héloïse. Marianne has been hired to secretly paint Héloïse's portrait after she refused to sit for a former artist in order to delay an arranged marriage. It is Marianne's job to pose as Héloïse's companion by day and to paint her portrait from memory by night. Héloïse is cloaked at first—face coverings, hood, darkness, emotionless—so Marianne studies her through these veils. The first portrait she completes is stiff, *capturing* her subject.

> Héloïse says, *Is that me?*
> *Yes.*
> *Is that how you see me?*
> *It's not only me.*
> *What do you mean not only you?*

There are rules, conventions, ideas.
You mean there's no life? No presence?
Your presence is made up of fleeting moments that
may lack truth.
Not everything is fleeting. Some feelings are deep.
And after a pause Héloïse adds,
The fact it isn't close to me, that I can understand.
But I find it sad it isn't close to you.

As the scene closes, Marianne smudges the face into a ghostly apparition.

Once I started to face myself, the messages my body spoke to me became clear. Tracing through frozen shoulder, chronic pain, and anxiety, I separated from my partner of thirteen years, separated from my chosen family, tightened boundaries from my biological family, learned to disappoint my students at the university, and moved to a new city. In this solitude, I float and listen. My senses guide me, and the hollow feeling of living a secret has dissolved. The loneliness of living inside the narrative of others—even those who loved me well—is dissipating. I am alone but not lonely.

face, from *fro—I speak, I talk, I say*. Descendant of *faerie* and *fadude*, to become.

Pre, from *prae—in front of* or *before*.

That which comes before the magic of becoming. That which is said before I speak.

How much is to be said before I say anything? How will you know I love you even when I know I'll lose you? So much of connection is built with a goodbye, including loving yourself.

Fady Joudah in "Venus Cycle" writes,

> *Was I ever a moth*
> *or you this kind of light?*
>
> *One of us was dying, and one*
> *had no wings for the journey back.*

This is how I want to write this book: to say it all before it is said.

TRANSANYTHING

TRANSANYTHING

TIDE

What T wants my words to be: bristle sword fern, nettle stung tongue, sunk saguaro need/le, lists in texture, anything penetrating

What T wants my chest to be: tide knife, surf push, wave lash, pink time tether between gender

What T wants my paintings to be: matte black dusk, charcoal edge of world, neon five layers under

What T wants my belly to be: hip shift, saunter, sauté, give way, stubborn estrogen committee of executives

What T wants my voice to be: spit jowl, feral fang above whisper, long cedar tone—a reckoning, nocturnal claw cascade

What T wants my body to be: woodpecker prophetic charge, that winter the wolf came, thorn procession of potential holy harm

Double-knitted over E, or cloudful eclipse. Only synonym with an unbeginning, or a phase in spectrums.

Declension, decline, degeneracy, degradation, devolution—gatherings of losses from a certain peak. Instead: The what that always was, cover the vacuum hose with one finger and the splaying of suction. Less descension, more ebbing in the bend.

The gender bend is delicate, amorphous—a sinking and float. Every day, carrying out, then the dredge and what returns. How much of me returns to myself when I pull the covers up at night? Where are the sifted pieces, the dust of a self contorted under every gaze—in what state do I return from your eyes making shapes of me?

MYSTIC SURGERY I

Surgery comes from hand, not surge as in *surgere*, to rise and fall, or swell with great force. Work done by hand, as in stitching, sewing, washing—the rise and fall of needle or sock into serge.

My top surgery was a bilateral mastectomy with nipple grafts. I was left to imagine the process: scalpel in his gloved hands   seven-inch curved openings cut near the imagined male chest line   seven straight lines sliced around the crooked circle of each areola   lift and removal of each areola on silver tray   cut out each nipple   removal of milk duct   trim nipple revision   stitch to minimized areola   removal of breast tissue   (I still can't imagine this part)   pull down loose skin flaps and stitch   cut hole for reconstructed nipple and areola   (imagine star-shaped cookie cutter here)   stitch on areola   wash, wrap chest.

NIPPLE AESTHETIC

Blood-crusted pennies, rustic blouse buttons, hutch handles, butch knuckles, dry-ink thumbprint, rusted bottlecap, sunset flower stigma, lunar eclipse with an almost-goodbye; their red ochre alizarin weight, marigold pollen smudge, jellyfish disk, worm in spiral, earth-pulling sun horizon, glitter circle in amorphous bend, retired hermit shell, areolar trim and heap on a new boychest.

MYSTIC SURGERY 2

Once my chest skin produced enough healing tissue to bubble into scar, I stopped sleeping through the night. On my side of the bed, the burgundy back pillow took the impression of my spine. My shoulders relaxed as my arms dangled over the armrests and the tight chest bind squeezed my ribs. One night I awoke with the distinct impression that spirits were healing my chest—the place under the scars and empty space of tissue. Spirits, ancestors, angels—I will never name them, but every night that winter I quietly gathered with the surgeons in the dark, the house asleep while they performed their invisible work. The elation and awe beyond any word fixed and interpreted by time.

The first time I saw a river empty into ocean I sensed two branches of planetary water jaggedly riffing. The Atlantic Ocean seemed a colonizing surge, the Cape Fear River the sustaining shores of trade and capital, particularly the revenue from selling and trading African people. I knew there was more to the story then—the earth's history and Indigenous civilizations far predate colonization, but in the diagonal clash of river and ocean all I could see that day was the swallowing of the river's soul.

What I was witnessing was flow: river flowing to ocean, ocean ebbing and flowing—that continual drain and rise. When I was a child growing up in Massachusetts, I remember visiting the Museum of Science in Boston twice, both times pausing a long time at the reconstructed hydraulic tank of ebb and flow. In that long, snaking cylindrical tank wrapping around the wall, I felt somehow the wholeness of being alive. I did not understand it all; just the way water rushed and returned. These two phases never entirely complete.

FLOW 2

Thirty-one months after my breasts were hollowed and shaped into masculine-appearing pecs, I cannot remember my breasts. I want to write *those* breasts, because it seemed like someone put them there—they never really were mine.

What I do remember: pulling a T-shirt on the first time after they were gone, my breath clear and wide, canyon wind; buttoning up my postsurgical flannel, smoothing the seams and buttons like a lover's collar; reaching in my dresser drawer for underwear and socks and feeling the somatic tightening in my chest as I reached for a sports bra I would no longer need.

To what degree can I accept that those breasts were never mine and never really there? Dysphoria an ebbing of reality—the what that always was, the vacuum hose shifting suction, or sucking air in a new direction. I never spoke my breasts alive, never admitted them. They seemed there by the eyes of others, not my own. What to say of reality undefined, undetermined?

Days after recalling the hydraulic tank at the Museum of Science, fish appeared. There were fish in the tank, washing back and forth in the tide's ebb and flow. Two fish with silver, articulate eyes stayed near me in the flow. Faith in the ebb and dredge to bring nutrients to bear.

Black lipstick epistle, gem-crusted jellyfish bell, bioluminescent sundial of tides, nipple nestle, chest trestle, sea star constellation fugitive, foxglove cat paw, wolf hackle in incremental wound, stitch scar in ocean heal, willow wrap, diva snap, ruby glitter hummingbird, its sky zipping and dips, its tongue coil snaking around skull, nectar manifest, heels clicking.

FLOW 3

It took forty-three years to understand I was trans without hormones to justify it, so trapped I was in the binary. The binary is an imposed heartbeat, it is layered over us again and again. Its robotic pulse is like a never-changing tide placing the same shells on the same part of the shore day after day until the shells run out. No one swims anymore—they float, complacent in the othering of a usual current. Any heartbeat is far from robotic—it shifts, responds, adapts to its situation. It's how an animal knows it's in danger or safe; it's how the body responds to safety and excitement—even love is recorded in the heartbeat. Pulse, heart rhythm, the energy field of anything alive—these are the natural regulators. They learned to sway and skip with the planet and universe. Scientists are beginning to understand that Earth's heart beats every twenty-seven million years. Imagine the tiny happenings in our bodies as geologic forces shift.

SURGE

I noticed it first in my throat, like testosterone slowly plunged a voice deeper in my chest. My voice. But other—like every word shaded in some other life. I worried my throat would close completely; my words capsized, lost under the swell. Next, my jaw settled somehow, and the upper lip hairs deepened toward mustache whiskers. I bought a razor and shaving cream at Target, determined to control the flow of changes. My clitoris swelled with energy, nearly stealing my voice that summer—directing my attention toward impulse and desire. I drew back, back as far as I could, not touching until I had to. I was terrified of becoming weaponized; another man wielding seed. I told my therapist *I don't want to become a weapon.*

What top surgery dredged: hardened silica, terse diamond spikes, shoulders like two phantom limbs caught in their sockets. It felt at times like I didn't belong in my body, or that my life was at war with its future. Frozen shoulder paralyzed me into a pause.

UNRAVELING I

A knot has two parts: weaver and thread. A weaver can be a spider, wind, human, idea—any force to interlace two ends of a body. The knot is the imposed agreement of the body or bodies, where they intersect and bind: lump, mound, clump—all of this according to the weaver's design.

The morning I slapped testosterone gel onto my shoulders I knew I'd chosen to wade into an unwoven current—one characterized by a preternatural force. The gel was cool and slathered around, sloppy like aloe after sunburn. It soaked into my shirts and left a sticky skein on my skin. As I increased the dose, applying the gel reminded me of the children's show where, if you guessed the wrong answer, you'd be humiliated, covered in slime. In spring 2020 I was forty-three, the design of the world severed—an unraveling; a swift pause on a still-spinning planet; and I slipped into the pause to find myself.

Before a spider weaves, it uses gravity or wind to carry an anchor line. In its abdomen, silk is forged into a clump between its fourth legs. The spider drops the silk ball to catch on a leaf or sails it into a breeze—a seed, a messenger.

My brother Joe and I grew up in a family shaped by tangled sorrow. My mother's manic depression and schizophrenia wove a blanket of fear and uncertainty around us. She would be hospitalized in a sanatorium when I was eight, a time I remember roller-skating precisely along the tar stripes stitching the streets together. A time of swinging hinges: the side-door hinge at Grandma's house in Ohio, the fence hinge, the garage-door hinge—all violently swung open. Shortly before I was born, a back injury forced my dad to leave construction work for a stable career in the Army, whose framework for a soldier and his family is fracture. We never knew where we would live or for how long. Never knew when we would be estranged from my dad for another three-month field training. Never knew who would catch us when Mom finally fell apart. Sorrow and fear seeped bone deep. My body still holds the shape of someone just departed, hips twisted one way to run, shoulders twisted another way to stay.

IN THE STANCE OF SOMEONE JUST DEPARTING

9:18 A.M.
In the stance of someone just departing, the wolf's body is gently askew. The body. The body is grounded at the chest but light as wings in the lungs.[1]

9:19 A.M.
In the stance of someone just departing, two paws tightly wind springs holding ground, two corresponding paws poise to lift.[2]

---

1. *All eyes, the creatures of the World look out / into the open. But our human eyes, / as if turned right around and glaring in / encircle them; prohibiting their passing.* —Rainer Maria Rilke, *The Duino Elegies*

2. *What lies outside, their faces plainly show us. / Yet we compel even our youngest; force / each child always to stare behind, at what's / already manifest . . .*

9:20 A.M.

In the stance of someone just departing, the ears rotate around sound waves coming from the highway, all its rumbling and clunky lightning.[3]

9:21 A.M.

In the stance of someone just departing, the body's wet nose takes in streams of scents: the sweetness of last night's elk, raw stench of last week's kill by the river, warm last notes of a raven's life, human bodies along the highway, human chips, human coffee, human coffee cake, human bread, human's thin slices of turkey and cheese, human hot dog.[4]

9:26 A.M.

In the stance of someone just departing, the ginger-furred body eases down near a broad stripe of sagebrush.[5]

9:27 A.M.

In the stance of someone just departing, the left ear flicks away a black horsefly buzzing the sounds of torn paper in its ear.[6]

---

3. . . . *and not to see / that openness which lies so deep within / the gaze of animals.*

4. *Animals / keep death behind them, and before them, God.*

5. *We never have, not for a single day, / pure space before us—all its flowers / opening endlessly.*

6. *And yet, sometimes a silent animal / looks up at us and silently looks through us. / We call it Fate to be in opposition. / Nothing but that. Forever opposite.*

9:34 A.M.

In the stance of someone just departing, the body moves in its unison of parts behind the slope of sagebrush, and on up into the hills of the Lamar Valley.[7]

9:35 A.M.

In the stance of someone just departing, a bodied animal was under the human gaze.[8]

It is a wolf in early light, a distant hunting party streaming down dimming green hills, it is a herd of bison gathered on ground nearer to stars, pronghorn deer skirting the rims of a canyon, a mule deer vanishing to the creek's edge, it is the marmot in their tunnels, the red fox lunging at underground sound, it is the way the hawk wing folds around the body, it is the bighorn sheep curling its horns against pitch pine, scratching a seashell into the bark, it is the shell against the ear, the raven disappearing into the universe of sky, the beaver in its den of sticks and mud, coyote in sagebrush plateau, elk in their mystical circles at the forest edge cloaked in the ancient steam of a geyser, it is

---

7. *To animals / their being is infinite, unknowable; / and they look out from it, not at themselves. // And where we see future, they see the whole; / Themselves within it; held and healed forever.*

8. *And we, we stay spectators; turned towards / all things and still transcending none. / All overwhelms us. We set all in order. / All falls apart. We order it once more / and fall, collapse, disintegrate ourselves.*

humans on the roadside wanting to see, wanting so badly to see something, wanting to catch a wolf and swallow its feral moonlight into the marrow of their bones.[9]

9. *Who has turned us around like this, so that / always, no matter what we do, we're in the stance / of someone just departing? As he, / on that last hill that shows him all his valley / one last time, turns, stops, lingers—, / we live our lives, forever taking leave.*

LONELY SPECIES

C made me ears from old suede gloves the color of charred brimstone. They pasted fake sheep's wool in the center, an illusion of depth. I glued the ears to cardboard and pinned the ensemble to a headband.

Hearing seared me; my neighbor's spit dissolving venison between his teeth, the cat on the first floor breathing on the window, a rustle in the crisp leaves below the old alder across the way.

I robed my neck in a fur stole, painted my face with whiskers, felt a coarse growl fill the low space of my throat. Just under my chin I fastened the GPS tracking collar, a hand-forged mechanism made from a headlamp and tinfoil. I left quietly, a cloud slipping over the moon.

Today, I measured distance from a certain point: N 36°7'44", W 121°37'4", a cliff in the Santa Lucia Mountains. I rose when the flickers left their nest a few yards from our Airstream. Their sweet-pitched *kyeer* flushed the air sienna above their spotted breasts. Chatter of the first birds already woke up the canyon, but we waited in the half light of morning while the black-capped chickadees chortled in the dry branches of the sycamore. This was right before the crickets quit their humming, just before the sun reached the crest of the Santa Lucias, just after the planet spun us away from the full body of our only moon and the stars became the idea we leave them to be when we are not looking.

The jays heard us first, I think, and brought their dry *caw* to our doorstep. The air in their throats a rusty door creaking open as we lit the stove burner with a spark. We heard the heavy fog unfurl from the Pacific, flooding the canyon into silhouettes of shapes like sheets drying in the sun. Seconds after, light warmed the flutes of fuchsia, the ruby-throated hummingbird looped down to its core. Nature's performance fused to my body through my eyes and tongue, through the shifting birdcalls drumming my anvils into recognition and the sun turning the mist against my skin into heat-cracked rock.

Distance may be a condition, an interval, a length. An avoidance, a space, reticence. An aloofness from the equator intersecting an aloofness from Greenwich, England. *Where am I?* the coordinates ask.

You are here, my dear, you are here.

But where is that?

Loneliness, too, is distance: a condition, a length, an interval between body and experience; aloofness from the present moment. I am writing this, so I am lonely: my senses on pause so my mind can move through the space of memory. You are reading this, so perhaps you, too, are lonely.

A lone wolf settles for a moment under a shade tree in a tuft of June grass, sniffing miles of breeze. *Lone* leans on cliché, the myth of the isolated wolf howling on the periphery of what we see and know. Here we make a distinction between isolated and lonely: the wolf seeks a companion from the wiring of his senses. The DNA map of his species whispers through his spine: *find. a. mate.* He uses his nose, ears, tongue, the gallop of his paws grabbing miles. The wolf is fully embodied. He will not rest until he finds a mate and will tear the flesh and muscle of rabbit and deer to sustain his journey.

Our human loneliness, on the other hand, is a state of being that distances us from our bodies. We are more surrounded than ever by our own species, we are loved and comfortable, yet we are catastrophically lonely.

The day C and I left the honeymoon Airstream nestled on the cliff, our host drove us down his long driveway, a dirt path winding along a ridge overlooking Highway 1 and the Pacific. I rode in the back of the truck with Piha, a protective and affectionate gray dog who sprang into the truck bed on cue. Her archaic canine jaws snapped at branches that lined the driveway, peeling off leaves and stems; a sensuous form of trimming the hedges, I supposed. Our host Richard invited us to come back, maybe live and work the land for a season if our schedules cleared up. I think he meant: *If you can figure your lives out*, or: *If you're willing to risk transformation from your life in the city.*

We told him goodbye and sat in our car, an unfamiliar rectangle of metal and plastic.

C said, *I miss you.*

I said, *I miss you already, too.*

That's when the measurements began. We stopped in Monterey (N 36°36'85", W 121°53'40") for fuel, watching the California coast slip past us. My seat belt crossed my neck in a suffocating twist as we passed highway construction and cars from all over the West. I suddenly wanted to stop at a bakery. I suddenly wanted cake. I suddenly wanted a latté. I suddenly wanted to fill myself with stuff. I was becoming lonely.

We spent the day in San Francisco, about 1° farther north and 73° more west, to stay with C's brother. We ate a spread of tapas, talked about the sun and birds and quiet in the past tense, and slept in a teenager's bed that smelled like the loneliness of a boy who lives most of his life attached to a computer. Our bodies were a seam, pulling slightly apart from each other.

No one understood my costume. In fact, no one even asked about it. It was warm in the bar, and I could smell my body's nervousness as I looked at slutty vampires, femme fairy-tale princesses, and masculine superheroes numbing themselves with whiskey and beer. I was introduced to read my poems and my body tightened. The GPS collar gripped me snugly, its two red lights beaming eyes at the audience.

Holy holy land of the hunt, holy holy powder keg, I read.

The only wild wolf in California goes by two names: OR-7 and Journey. The first name was created by scientists to categorize the wolf, alluding to the Inmaha pack's origin in Oregon, while Journey came from the imagination of two children—"Name the Lone Wolf of California" contest winners. You can imagine the submissions: Night Traveler, Moon Howler, Wayward Wolf, Inspiration, Lonely Hunter. But Journey captured the essence of this wolf who broke with his pack to travel south to Siskiyou County, to crisscross the invisible border into California, then ultimately head homeward to Oregon.

Journey isn't nature's name, but it does rest in metaphor and myth: casting a hero who beats the odds against otherworldly protagonists; Odysseus on the hull of a ship following starlight, colonial settlers establishing a city on the hill, Luke Skywalker manifesting his destiny. *Journey* reaches out to our imaginations, though it is a word rooted in a day: a day's portion of life. Only later did journey take on a lifetime. A term of time undeterminable and lonely.

What then for our western wolf who wanders and settles territory by senses rather than language? Whose urine and olfactory sense are his language of identification? Colonizers journeyed to what would become the western United States as protagonists, then eradicated the wolf (antagonist). Perhaps now the roles have shifted: our lone wolf as protagonist, on a journey to rediscover the West.

I've always felt uncomfortable with naming. My college writing instructor, Elizabeth Dodd, professed the importance of learning names. *Learn the birds!* she exclaimed in deft assonance. But I was a painter then, working abstractly. I wanted essence by way of lyricism, not representation. I needed so badly to feel something, that the distance created by language was unbearable. American finch vs. cedar waxwing held no magic in those days, so locked I was from my body.

So how can we even regard a name for *Canis lupus*, whose jaws clench enough force to break bone, whose howls travel through octaves for fifty miles? Who fills human imaginations with terror and heart and moon song? The gray wolf is the very essence of wild that cannot be contained by representation.

In the only photograph of him, he follows the trail of a mate invisible now for ninety years. He is nearly imperceptible in the green and purple grasses of a California meadow.

The effect is a Monet painting of impressionistic light and color. If you didn't know to look, you might miss it.

I once felt a wolf attach to me, so I followed it. C had shown me an article in *The New York Times*, "'Famous' Wolf Is Killed Outside Yellowstone." In the photograph of 832F, the wolf's belly is a study of whites against the early winter snow of Yellowstone, her back a mottled gray granite. She stands alert, curious, perhaps playful, next to 754, a wolf from her pack killed a month earlier. She was the alpha female of her pack, which roams the lower Lamar Valley, an area heavy with human tourism. There is no fence around the park, it simply eases into the landscape that is named public land. She was killed on the wrong side of it, her $4,000 GPS collar a silver can slumped in the snow.

I woke up and she was there, a warmth by my right ear, her presence attached to me. I can only say that she needed help, that she wasn't going to let go until I helped. I dragged myself to my desk and began to write.

A New England blizzard piled over three feet of snow on the region. I was five, so the snow towering above me became the world. I scooped the powdery crystals in my palm and held all of existence there for a time. I wondered if this was magic.

And this: the palm, and how it holds the world roundly: rocks, jacks, dice, dirt, bowl, water from the sink or a muddy puddle in southern Ohio that I thought was the sky. My mother's palms lifted me under the hard bone of my sacrum and the fragile arc of my cervical spine. I don't remember this, but when anyone's palm cups my neck my nervous system eases and I still.

We arrived home in Seattle (N 47°37'8", W 122°18'30") the following day, after a ninety-seven minute flight from San Francisco that was delayed twenty-four minutes from the heavy drape of summer fog. We had stretched over N 11° and W 1° from Richard, Piha, and the Airstream on the Santa Lucia cliff. We said three sentences as we shot along I-5 toward home. A friend had assembled us a gift basket of local, organic foods to ease our return (two apples, one yogurt container, twelve ounces of granola), but the lonely city rose before us anyway, thousands of mirrored squares reflecting the clouded sky we had come to know. My body tightened under the angles, my jaw slipping into a rigid pattern. The vulnerability of my body covered in measures of glass, plastic, and metal.

To catch a wolf is to capture an idea of wildness buried in the physiology of our bodies. Every quarter I ask my environmental writing students, *Do you feel you are an animal?* At eighteen or twenty-one, it seems that most don't. Some say they are God's children, separate and in charge of caring for animals. Others suggest that their consciousness separates them from animals. Many just don't comprehend the question. This is a "good question," I tell them. One that leads to deeper conversations about science, religion, and philosophy. What I don't tell them is that we learn good questions to understand our lives until the day comes when we realize that questions never end. Language is like the galaxy and questions are hot air balloons floating into the ever-expanding future, which we can only imagine. So, we ask more questions, send up more balloons, until we're left realizing that time constantly moves away from us. We are grasping the invisible, living our entire lives in the realm of mystery, a place where the body is a carrier of myriad unknowns. And in this way, I suppose that I am teaching my students to suffer, or, at best, to be aware of their own suffering.

Despite colonial structures that have remained and expanded, reinforced so many lives into rigid lines, there are still connections that resist loneliness: the sun's measured appearances, the moon's shadow and glow, the woman who always says hello when you walk by, the unexpected heat when you first meet a special person, the seasons. Crimson maple leaves force heavier coats and wool socks. The violet crocus makes its annual February promise of spring and light. Only through perception do we experience loneliness from these constant companions.

I sometimes still grieve the return to Seattle. Longitude and latitude are minimal now: home, work, grocery store. N 47°37'8", W 122°18'30" are less a distance from California, and more a measurement of memory stored in the muscles of my body. Every northern flicker is morning fog unfurling, every match is a morning I remember with C when we were connected by our very presences. Here at N 47°37'8", W 122°18'30" I witness our slow pull from each other; phone calls, emails, text messages, work, friends, goals. We still turn to each other every night, our eyes warm with love, yet quick with the loneliness from our own bodies.

After the Halloween reading, I walked my neighborhood alone to see the late crowd of trick-or-treaters—teenagers, mostly, crawling along the streets, slithering between car bumpers covered with smeared moths. The moon hung as an anchor above, and not one costumed human checked their phone. The lights of my collar shone like eyes behind the dense cedars of the forest as I smelled the air for the wild nature of life.

PAPERCLIP: A STORY OF INVASIVE SPECIES

They appeared slowly at first from the neat container in my backpack: a thin one clipping assignments, a heftier clip to bind my students' poems making meaning from simple objects. They grew in numbers, spilling over, forming silver nets in my pockets. They claimed the covers of notebooks, fish-hooked the seams of my button-downs, embroidered shirt cuffs, collars; I even found one fastened to my watch-band, pinching a riverbed into the mud-brown leather. They swirled like good ideas in the washing machine, spreading like unfortunate pop songs, transforming each aspect of myself into clipped wings. They became invasive.

A naturalist and an ecologist walk into a bar. The naturalist says *I'll have a tap beer*, then sighs, watching the golden stream of lager languish in the glass, tracing drips of beer down the drain into a swirling world of fluids in the sea. The ecologist sits down, her stool wobbly, and says *Let me fix this stool.* She notices the floor is in disrepair and gets out the sanding stone. After examining the slant of the floor for some time, recording angles and the certain geometries of light, she says *I'll have a whiskey. Make it a double.*

In the subtle, green hills of Vermont, I took a walk with a naturalist and an ecologist. The morning's mist dampened the spirits of the black flies that had swarmed us a day ago, leaving us porous ground to walk on and perching wood toads to discover in the resident ponds. Every aspect of the forest felt like a resident, the moss resting on the lichen resting on the spruce roots, an ear of oyster mushroom listening to the cacophony of this place through its scalloped underbelly. Every aspect felt resident—except for us. They agreed that though the golden honeysuckle was invasive, its sweet drop on the tongue made it neutral. They shifted their sights instead to kudzu, nowhere to be found here in the Green Mountains.

The naturalist, Gary, sang the wonders of kudzu, its medicinal value for the skin, the liver, how as a tonic it eases allergies and the nervous system. To hear Gary talk about kudzu was to hear a stone monastery of voices chant to Lakshmi, the stone humid with their voices. He said a field overgrown with kudzu is a gift to the land, a bandage necessary to repair what has been broken. Leave it alone.

Julianne, the ecologist, zipped her fleece a little tighter, asked questions at first. If something is broken, and you broke it, don't you feel responsible to repair it? Isn't it our responsibility to fix the ecology of land and water? Destroy the kudzu, she implied, and restore the land to its natural balance before colonizing plants.

Paperclips create order by binding together sequences or holding stacks of similar pages together. They epitomize constraint in the tough, flexible metal that traps papers between their rounded teeth. Paperclips are problem solvers, more subtle than binder clips, less bulky than folders, far more flexible than a staple permanently etched into a corner. Paperclips are useful until you yourself are bound.

A poet walks into the bar carrying five dollars and a single paperclip. The poet sits at the bar, places the paperclip on the uneven, sticky wood. As they repeatedly stick and unpeel the paperclip from the drying orb of alcohol and cola, they begin to describe the paperclip's curve; how it bends twice so perfectly, how one bend is slightly longer than the other, how the metal is pliable, like their childhood, unbending and reshaping to meet their geography, their mother's moods. They reflect how they can never quite find the paperclip's original shape, their shape; just an echo of its natural form. The bartender buys them a beer. A dark one.

UNRAVELING II

A Darwin's bark spider (*Caerostris darwini*) builds a web across a river by beginning with a long anchor line. She sprays strands of silk in a continuous flow, like silly string carried by the wind above the river's surface. It is an act with knots in its design. As the silk sprays, she uses her legs to mass and tangle the threads together near her abdomen every few seconds. Too thin and the anchor line will break.

Billy-Ray Belcourt of Driftpile Cree Nation writes, "The body is a riddle and bones comprise a kind of orthography," in a poem whose title is its question: "What Is a Human Possibility?" (*The Ex-Puritan*, 2018). The poem's opening contrast of possibility and bone opens an original space to think into. If bones are an orthography, I feel the ache and moan of their spelling; a grammar of ventricle meaning-making singing the body into shape. The riddle is the impossible question, and its answer is found in human possibility. That the body is shaped and molded, massed and unraveled—a book of history and its unweaving. Belcourt continues, "I plucked the wings from my own back. / What I do not want stolen from me I destroy."

In spring 2020 I was ready to be a different question: no longer the queer woman the world thought I was and something more like the queer man I was not sure I intended to be. I wanted a new, original between-space, be it shadow or sun.

In the first weeks of T, I felt a sudden determination sink beneath my skin. My face didn't shift exactly, but no longer looked the same in photographs—like the camera knew to look at me in a new way.

What does it mean to speak the body? To pronounce its skeletal moans into a question? I sometimes interpret these mysteries as loneliness, but I also wonder whose loneliness it could be. In another poem Belcourt describes days when he feels like his body is anchoring him "in a world in which native means lonely and lonely feels a lot like dying." The colonial gaze, with its unlimited prescriptions of white supremacy and heteronormativity, brings the damage, but it's the body that inhabits and passes on the wound.

When preparing paper for watercolor, I often press the end of a paintbrush handle into the paper, making near-invisible designs. The impressions surge the paint into and away from the paper's valleys, serving as a kind of fingerprint design. These initial marks determine all that will be built upon them and all that will be sacrificed in the design.

On the other side of the river, shadows are apparitions, that subtle waving of darkness from the between spaces—places I refer to as the unbetween because each space is original, shifting; begging for imagination. It's funny how we watch shadows move, when really it is the light coming through that is the primary figure. On the other side of the river, the silk spray reaches through shadows near the shore, catches on a leaf. She has built an eighty-foot bridge to the other side and will quickly reinforce the anchor line with more silk. If the line breaks, she will gather it back using the hooks on her legs, then consume it.

SNAP THE WHIP

Through the window is the magnolia tree, but I only know it through reflection. The backdrop is the upper portion of a brick-red house, its columnar chimney like a skyscraper from this perspective. Magnolias bloom twice each year in this part of North Carolina, the fall and spring. The blossoms unfold white bundles of clean slates that spread open like a deck of cards. There's a trick there: now you see it, now you don't; a branch only hangs on for so long, then lets the flower go. Nothing in Wilmington seems to die the way I expect it to.

The landscape is laid perfectly over this screen where my words appear: brick triangle interrupted by tall rectangle, obscured by flat leaf patterns which sometimes move, all this framed by a window, all that framed by my laptop screen. This is how I prefer to write: laying letters across an already finished canvas. One thought on top of another, tangling realities into DNA strands that—twisted together like a wind chime in a storm—create an unexpected music: something like meaning.

My parents' home in Kansas is held together by habits. My dad has woken up at the same time every morning during their thirty-six-year marriage. In cold months, he puts on a robe that is identical to the first robe my mom ever bought him; rusted burgundy, soft material, not too thick. He goes to work after cold cereal and coffee while Mom sleeps late into the morning. The first time they see each other will be six o'clock in the evening.

I am wary of returning home after three years. I sit in a blue airport chair trying to invest some attention in a newspaper, but fidget instead with my nails and the silver zippers on my backpack. Will my parents look old? Will I fall back into my familiar family role? I feel I might be losing something. I gently bend my metal-rimmed glasses at the nose, and they noiselessly snap into two pieces in my hands, leaving me to travel home with little to see but what's right before me.

I read an article about a man who was murdered in Texas; his body was left to waste in New Mexico. It mentions little of his life, what he left behind. Did he have a close family? A wife? He worked as a restaurant executive, and I halt at the word *executive*, as it swerves dangerously close to *execute*: a word doubling over itself with heaviness. It comes to English in the twelfth century to mean "carry out, perform." One hundred years later, the term evolves: "to put to death." In 1776 American English applies the word to a judicial landscape: a person responsible for putting laws into effect. Executive and executioner; scissor blades fanning in and out from the handle.

In 1898, Wilmington was the largest city in North Carolina. It was wealthy and destined to fall apart. Cape Fear River snaked through the state and carved a port into the city, driving tobacco and lumber sales. The first Black lawyer in North Carolina lived and worked in Wilmington. The *Daily Record* was a small newspaper produced by the local Black community, printed in a house on Castle Street. Black people slowly built power, but this power had a trapdoor.

In November 1898, a white supremacist group gathered at the armory, marched downtown with guns and flags. They burned the Black printing press, killed Black citizens, overthrew local government. They ripped a seam through the city, leaving a wound that would never heal. Today, neighborhoods are segregated by race and poverty, and the Black middle class is very small. Many white citizens who seized the government have buildings named after them.

A former teacher of mine lives on Castle Street, across from the printing press. The building still retains burn marks and is littered with broken glass. The press is back up and running, but wary of people asking questions. My friend has an old door in her hallway. You can trace the smooth craters of bullet holes with your finger like a scar, sometimes seeing light through fractures.

I arrive in Atlanta for a brief layover and can see only shapes. The flight departures are written imperceptibly small and are listed fifteen feet from the ground, so I ask a man to please check my flight for me. He has on a red sweater, which seems festive, and I assume he is friendly. My dad calls and says that the roads in Kansas might be icy and that he will keep me updated. The roads in Kansas are usually icy in winter, the landscape bleak. The brown lends new meaning to brown. There's uncanny silence before movement, and always the silence after.

When an event becomes forgotten, the language shifts. The massacre—anywhere from twenty-two to hundreds of Black casualties—has historically been called a race riot and is just recently being relabeled a coup d'état. The change in language apparently being more accurate and appealing: the coup d'état in Wilmington was the only successful one in United States history, and this is how the history books will now write it: a struggle predominantly about government power rather than racial tensions. *Colpus* is Latin, a blow with the fist.

A man, fifty-five years old, drives out to the New Mexico desert. A landscape nearly invisible at night; cacti poking at stars, the rolling land buffeted by unexpected plateaus. He pulls his car over, probably a black or silver SUV with a Texas license plate, in a place far from city lights, miles from the truck stop, but not far from the road. He wants to be found. After twenty paces, he ties knots around the trigger. The helium balloons should be just strong enough. He points to the back of his head, balloons pull the gun into the atmosphere, blotting stars while leaning into dry, desert wind.

Murder is public because the factors are out of control of the victim. Someone is to blame, and answers are sought out. Suicide, however, is solitary. Its complication is privately resonant because it exists within itself, inside itself. It is a self-choice, similar to the way getting up in the morning is a choice. I had a conversation with a roommate once about suicide. I lay on the cold, wood floor staring at the ceiling, needing, I suppose, openness to consider the impulse. Her father was schizophrenic. He had committed suicide eight years ago. He died at his job—a school—and he too wanted to be found. My mother, also schizophrenic, has survived at least one attempt. After a troubling phone call that morning, I worried it would happen again, so I lay on my roommate's floor staring at her ceiling. The people who lived here before us had stars stuck to the white ceiling, which now existed only as sticky circles. Centers left behind from the glue, carved points removed, inexact.

My family lived twice in Arizona. The first time was when I was eight and everything was falling apart—the day my brother fell from his bicycle into the drainage ditch is a surreal memory, one that—visually—fits together: brother is around the corner, I turn corner, brother ascends from the ditch without bike, has goose egg on forehead, brother cries, I get Mom for help, everyone goes inside the house. But emotionally I can't understand how it all happened. How my brother could have been so helpless. How angry and out of control my mother looked. Why didn't he carry his bike out from the ditch? Why did he feel guilty for falling?

I unclick my seatbelt in unison with the other passengers; the moment just before the cabin door opens. The sound is a line of dominoes falling into each other; chain reactions of moments setting the future in motion. I walk out of the terminal and look for the shape of my parents: tall, lanky father standing to the right of my mother, heavy with weight and self-doubt. Their faces imaginary until I step right up to them, not sure if the person I was on the plane reflected the one here, hugging my dad, watching my mom cry in relief, despair. Her eye shadow is lavender, our favorite color.

When I was in the third grade, my mom was descending into madness. My brother and I would cry at the dinner table if we detected any change in her mood. We didn't have language for her illness, only grief. My third-grade teacher gave us a project: tie a message to a balloon and send it into the sky. We were to learn, I suppose, the act of making something and letting it go. The act of wishing. I wrote a message for my family. I sent my message far up until it disappeared.

I saw *Snap the Whip* once at the Met. Winslow Homer painted the American pastoral the way Mark Twain wrote it. I had always wanted to feel the tension of the painting in person; the way two boys stand in the back, holding the line; another boy in a startlingly white shirt centers the break; a group of boys swing the momentum; two boys tumble into the ground. A human whip where each individual movement has a purpose in the motion—and when I saw the painting, I cried because there we all were. My father holding the line, my brother centering the break, me running ahead, my mother taking the fall. We are all there, and there are flowers and stones all around the frame.

Walking a short distance through New Mexico just off the interstate, someone sees a curious tangle around a cactus. Looking closer, strings are wound around the thorns on one arm of the cactus, where maybe once a wren's nest nestled inside. Maybe once an impossibly small beak broke the egg's shell. Attached to one end of the strings are deflated balloons, which at this point look like used socks. Dangling down the back of the cactus is a gun attached to the string. The man wanted to be found, but not found out.

And the sky. Through the leaves in the computer screen, dappled, waving, shifting, is the sky, which is a quiet, easy blue. I just tilt the lens up a bit, and it is there. All this happening underneath some version of it. Something just over every ridge—the landscape holding our losses.

I never stopped looking for the message. I knew that it fell somewhere: a balloon can only float so far. I biked through every street, walked into a multitude of deserts looking. I wanted my message back.

UNRAVELING III

I was living in South Seattle with my partner and chosen family, coparenting a toddler, when our lives became shuttered. It would be a near-global shuttering; a sudden global web whose anchor line—this "new normal"—would stretch across the planet. None of the old books on the shelf seemed to matter anymore except the ones telling the truth about the violent past or telling the truth about collapsing futures. Yet at the same time, Netflix and liquor stores became big-ticket items. The nation was swept away by *Tiger King* and *The Crown*. Not only did the British monarchy leap back into popularity in 2020, so did *Friends*, which was the eighth most-watched TV series on Netflix worldwide. What was it about these comforting structures drawing humans to the screen night after night? Maybe as our worlds become lonelier, we reach for familiarity, even when familiar things are poison.

I needed new words. The old ones in the old ways became useless—even those just written. I started a notebook, "Spring 2020." The first entry is an early collection of key pieces of language layering us over: pandemic, outbreak, vulnerable, virus, compromised, continuing, spread, rate of infection, rate of spread, rate of mortality, nurses, front line, quarantine, online, Zoom.

Items listed as "returning": dolphins, swans, balcony singing.

I was angry at my body then, but it was like anger with a stranger. Someone walking too slow, too lumbering. On page three of my notebook, I recorded that I'd developed two frozen shoulders a month before I started testosterone—first the left, then the right. My arm seized when I tried to lift it at the joint; I couldn't throw a cat toy down the hall without wincing in agony; couldn't get my keys from the hook or a coffee cup from the cupboard. The connective tissue in my shoulders tightened and squeezed until the joints immobilized—two giant knots of ligaments, tendon, and bone. At night, I'd sit up on my recovery pillow from top surgery two seasons before and wait a full hour until the pain dulled enough to sleep. I woke up at 5 A.M. every morning with the first light's first bird, always a robin once the warbler's nest was destroyed by a raccoon. One dawn I lay there sobbing as early-morning crows ambushed a robin's nest of nearly hatched eggs, tiny blue eggshell confetti marking the ground.

Once the anchoring line is attached, the spider will pace that line again and again, fortifying it with silk. It is not until that line is solid that the spider begins to weave its pattern. She weaves outward from the anchor, generating more lines to the web than she will keep. Many spiders select seven primary lines around the anchor line, strengthening each with extra thread. This will be the spiderweb's blueprint.

I understand the body is composed primarily of liquid. I get that the body breathes and releases air. I know that atoms move in translational motion from one point to another; they vibrate and wiggle. I can articulate how a ball-and-socket joint works and stretching and yoga and memory and imagination. But to me, the body has always been a series of knots; tiny dams in the system. Gender is a hidden knot inside the body, a mass so lonely in its expression of blood and breasts that some days it feels like dying. When I was five, I remember looking down at my forearm thinking *what a great boy arm, I want to keep it.* At fourteen I scratched at a cut on my forearm for weeks, hoping for a scar. By fifteen I stopped trying, the knot pulled tightly. I crept into it.

If you grow up in a culture made of water, then you can transanything. To transanything is an inherent freedom to be alive; alive without legislature to make it possible; without economy to scratch a dividing line between gender; without the gaze to decide if you are safe. To transanything is a life without norms, a body without expectations; an anchor line before the weavers lock in a pattern you cannot exist in or exist without. Without transanything, society is dependent upon corporate sponsored prescriptions, social sponsored prescriptions, and legislative sponsored prescriptions. It forces queer and nonbinary people toward a binary and makes gender affirming health care a solution—a cure—a cure that you must depend upon even though the cure is controlled by poison.

In European languages *cure* is rooted in *care*—to take care of. To cura, care, cure meant to feel concern over another's spirit. Care, not solution—not fix. Only later did *remedy* appear; only after someone became a curer. Only after cure became owned, molded, controlled—another knot.

I like to think of the body being healed through being held. That when we care for each other we are curing each other. So much of my ancestry is rooted in Western European caste systems and settler colonial culture, and many members of my ancestry assimilated for survival. I don't have a clear portrait of care. Settler colonialism, white supremacy, patriarchy: these are the legends on the map I inherited. These are the weavers' knots designed to colonize what would become America. Knots that have been pulled and hardened by the paradigm of self-interest for centuries.

PAPER CRANES

Birds I've never heard before sing unfamiliar songs that sound like the fast, uneven revolution of a rusty wheel. I am 3,333 feet higher today than I was a week ago. These spinners of dusty tales whistle a heated exchange of aria and exhibition as jittery as a jingling chain in a storm. In the high country of Boone, North Carolina, spirits as alive as wind hover around the oaks, locusts, and poplars, and under the umbrellas of the river willows winding along the banks of the New River. This, one of the oldest rivers on the planet, lyrically courses through time.

Boone is surrounded by mountains and veined with rivers and belongs to the Cherokee and Watauga tribes. There's a reverence in the current settlers of this area—primarily white—though the reverence is based on the broken consciousness and unhistoried consequences of colonialism. Trappers and traders began to frequent the land in the 1500s, then came the gold seekers and with them the disease and greed and violence. Boone was named after Daniel Boone, and the town preserves his travels through the land in an annual historic reenactment. And, yes, there's a weird, giant statue near an old buffet-style restaurant. Today migrant mallards bask on giant gray stones in the ancient light behind my cabin.

Find the poison, you will discover its cure. There's a wives tale in the mountains that says a healing plant grows closest to what it will cure. I think this as I stare at a sturdy hardwood, measuring the rugged lines of bark leading to the top. Distinct yellow light sifts through the fractures of leaves. Joan Mitchell whispers to me through time, *the miracle*, she may have called this light as the sun looked down at her, as she stared up at a stand of *peupliers*, poplars outside Monet's old house in Vétheiul. I think this as mudslides take down the side of a mountain in Washington, burying lives on a Saturday morning, as oil settles into millions of tiny coffins along Louisiana and Alabama's shores. Roots of cure and poison tangle far below the ground where ants build their nations, nature's yin and yang reflected in the simple green of a weed.

When I was a child living in imagination, I was never a lifeguard or a nurse, not a firefighter or pilot or princess. I was a hero with magical powers. I was Adam thrusting my sword into the sky, gathering lightning bolts into electricity, claiming *by the power of Grayskull, I Have the Power!*— transforming into He-Man in moments. By the power of something that felt mythological, I was empowered to dream and explore with invincible cunning; a purple leaf was the key ingredient for a potion, a rock with gold flecks was omen; with the right combination of stones and leaves I solved complex riddles. I was Luke Skywalker with the innate sense of being one with the world, wielding an invisible force running through all living things.

Jewelweed is a medicinal herb that grows wild in these mountains. Yellow- and orange-spotted trumpets bloom like windsocks all over the hills. There's room in each horn-shaped flower for a crawl space for bees. Sunlight shines into the flowers, illuminating caverns of tiny leopard spots, red and brown stains like painted charcoal symbols from the past. Jewelweed and poison ivy grow in patches on the trails by my house. If you catch the rash from poison ivy before it spreads, jewelweed acts as a cooling elixir on the skin. Poison and cure. I imagine crawling onto the spindly center of the flower, wrapped in the petals of this mountain.

There's the saying, *She's not in her right mind.* This was something my Grandma Libby would say when my mother was acting crazy. *Don't worry, honey, she's not in her right mind today*, as she stroked my brown hair. I ate a soft chocolate chip cookie and tried to believe her, then went outside to weave through the tar-striped streets on my roller skates. The tar's pattern was a twisting meander, wide paths turning arcs like hawks that loop into each other. I pressed my thumb into the soft rubber until it gave then released. I pressed again, massaging the tar that held the ground together. None of us knew then about insanity. In the 1980s we couldn't reference Mom's symptoms on the internet and draw a hypothesis about schizophrenia. Instead, we separated into individual folds of fear, not knowing if we were Mom's poison, or if we could be her cure.

An origami crane has twenty-seven folds. The doorways and corners of Annie's apartment were each protected by a folded paper crane hanging by a string from a stick. Nine omens of peace and healing, 243 folds, creases of wings hovering in every corner. I was staying there for a few weeks, still wandering the air drafts of my early thirties. I carefully burned herbs throughout the apartment, creating a symphony of smoke until suddenly the dry leaves sparked and popped, sent burning ash toward my shirt and arm. I wasn't supposed to be there. I sensed that I was wrecking the system, disrupting the balance of light and dark held by the cranes—poison and cure fixed into a working grid.

When I was eight, Mom couldn't find her way back to her right mind. She was sent to Ohio to stay with her mother, a place she felt safe. Dad stayed behind to complete his military orders in Arizona while my brother and I boarded the plane with her, fought over the window seat and whose Dr. Pepper glass was fuller. The flight attendant gave us clip-on gold wings and told us we were the pilot's helpers. When his voice called out low and rumbly from the speakers, we knew he was talking to us.

At Grandma's, she screamed, pounded her fists on the table. Her eyes were dark, wild as a shifting wheat field before thunder. Black as deep night. She hated her house, her dead father; no one understood what she saw; she slammed the gate to the wire fence, bending its hinges in a permanent fold, saying that doctors would cut off her legs and I shouldn't want them to do that to her. I stood in a kind of silence impermeable by time. I stayed there for twenty years.

The early meaning of *right* began as adjective: straight, lawful, genuine. The word quickly developed into a verb: "to make right; to straighten out." Twenty-seven folds, crease with your fingertip, press firmly.

Each teaching of the Noble Eightfold Path in Buddhism begins with the word *right*. Right view, right intention, right speech, right action, right livelihood, right effort, right mindfulness, right concentration. *Right*, in this case, means togetherness or coherence. Each teaching is like a spoke on the Dharma Wheel, leading the way out of suffering. Right mind: right mindfulness: *samyak-smrti*. In Buddhist teachings, right mindfulness refers to being present: when you brush your teeth, you concentrate on tooth brushing; when you eat cereal, you are not at the computer or speaking. Your mind is doing one thing at one time. My mom's mind was the opposite of this. The present moment was indecipherable; she heard nothing but poisonous thoughts and voices.

Before I left for Boone, leaving my coastal home of five years, a dear friend, Kate, gave me a paper crane for the journey. Folded from fragile, tissue-like paper from China, she said it was given to her a long time ago, and it was time for it to travel with me. Four months earlier, Kate and I were sharing painting time on a difficult Saturday afternoon. I told her that I wanted to live where the sky was green, that I was dreaming of a green sky—she turned her yellow and blue abstract into a green sky over gray hills and told me to never forget where I was going. Now, here in the land of a thousand greens—silver-tipped and blue—I have never felt more at home.

After Mom was hospitalized and released, my family moved to Massachusetts. My brother and I started school again, a time to forget about home, to play on the playground and get bruised like everyone else. I was the fastest kid in my grade. The boys would run out of breath before they could catch me; I was already unreachable, vowed to a familial silence. Mom stayed at home for a few years before going back to work here and there. She would cook our meals and watch TV with us most evenings. She cried when we didn't expect it, a sudden tear we saw from the corners of her eyes. I didn't know then that this was shame. Shame of her lack of control. Shame that she had let us down. I didn't know she wanted to be strong and sane for us while experimental anti-psychotics were working on her mind, trying to make it right.

Cranes are ancient birds, perhaps the *most* ancient bird on the planet. The Japanese crane stands at a glorious five feet, red crown resting on his white-plumed body. In Japan, the crane's lore reaches back through the oldest lineages of culture. A symbol of happiness and eternal life, cranes are a coveted species. Once, I came across a crane knee-deep in a swampy pool at Bradley Creek in Wilmington. He was lean and gray, magnificently tall. He walked with a slow lope and strut, exhibiting a kind of patient, conscious confidence. *Grus canadensis*, a sandhill crane taking a stroll in the moonlight of early dusk, silently watching with a still neck as I stood for a minute, then moved on, practicing my best impressions with each swagger.

I didn't know until I was twenty-three years old that I was terrified of becoming schizophrenic. I was shy. I knew there was a 50 percent chance. I had never told anyone that my mom was anything except "ill." I had buried the secret so deeply that I no longer knew it was there. A fifteen-year paralysis.

In the end, fascination would bring me back. A child looked at themselves in a puddle that sent ripples through their adult face, gathered their awe and spirit. *Fascinate*: to attract or hold attentively by a unique power—from Latin: "to bewitch or cast a spell on." I began to collect leaves, consciously drunk with curiosity, attentiveness, absolutely bewitched. When we are bewitched, we seem to love better, to tell everyone about our new findings with fervor and luminosity. We want to tell stories, act out a scene, or carve an idol of our new icon of discovery. We want to create.

Cranes are famous for their mating dances: hopping, wing display, twirling around each other. A pair of these birds engage in the dance, and for many cranes, it's a dance that lasts a lifetime. Many cranes partner for their entire lives, or at least live monogamously for many years. These dances are perceived as a dance of joy, an expression of love and life. It is no wonder that humans—whether at ceremonies, wedding dances, or just a group of lively nature observers with thin spectacles and a little too much wine in the canteen—embrace and embody these dances, reenacting them as embodied performance.

The origami crane, then, is a work of nature and logic. Origami is shaping something formerly un-alive into a three-dimensional representation of an object, person, place, or abstraction. Twenty-seven folds. Crane lore is pure magic.

Homer wrote of the powerful crane flocks who would migrate to the fields of Pygmies and try to take their land. In the *Iliad*, Homer described the *shriek of cranes flying to the world's end from the heavens. How the cranes bring death and doom to battling men.*

Pliny the Elder also added his pen to this tale, saying that Pygmies rode on rams and goats and fought against the cranes with arrows. There's another tale of Ibycus, a poet who was attacked by a thief. The cranes surrounded the thief until he confessed. My favorite is the story of cranes having a touchstone in their bodies that they could use to test gold if vomited up. I place my fingertip on the belly of the origami crane from Kate and sense the slightest ebb. Air, the touchstone of life, the crane's heavy wings carrying a spirit to heaven.

The most popular crane lore comes from Japan and tells how a crane lives for a thousand years. Fold a crane for every year of its life and receive a wish. It is common tradition to display a thousand folded paper cranes at a wedding for good luck. Twenty-seven hundred folds. There's the story of Sadako Sasaki: after being poisoned by radiation from the bombing of Hiroshima, she developed leukemia. Her wish was for health and recovery, so she started folding cranes—twenty-seven folds for each bird; the final touches to bend the neck, spread the wings. She completed six hundred and forty-four cranes before her death.

I've been reading about magic, but your father doesn't like me to talk about it, she says, laughing innocently. I imagine her sitting in her La-Z-Boy, one leg crossed over the other, which is rocking the chair front to back. She is wondering what I will say, if I will engage in this strand of conversation. My first thought is that she is going crazy again, spiraling into some abyss that only she can see. My second is that this will be a passing interest, and my third is that she is a very powerful woman and I should watch my step. My mom has always been uncannily psychic and sensitive. The lines blur between intuition and paranoia. So, I do what my father always does, I react with logic and reason. *There's a dark side to these things*, I say. *This is a path only to be taken with caution. We never know how far our thoughts can go.*

The practice of magic is very similar to prayer: to attempt to alter events by use of energy or spirits. A cauldron is not required, nor black robes or rhyming couplets with toads. To work *with* energy is simply a way of saying that you are alive. When we kick a ball, we work with the energy of our bodies to propel the ball forward. When we breathe quickly our energy speeds up; when we rest or meditate our energy slows down. Love is a form of energy with its own shape and intensity. So are colors. So are rocks. So is air. When we want or need something, when we are calling out to the gods for assistance, we are sending out our thoughts with the hope of being heard. We want something to happen. Whether we call it prayer or magic or manifestation, it is always about asking for help.

Vincent van Gogh's paintings embody the divide between control and chaos. In a famous self-portrait from 1889 we see his characteristically paranoid, withdrawn expression. The strokes of paint around Vincent's face are thin, frenetic, pulsating from the nerve centers below the skin. His jacket moves in waves and the background seems to flow in an energetic chaos that—because the entire portrait is painted blue—encompasses the man himself. The painting is flawless, the way the range of blues perfectly contrast the orange hues, the dark brows warily drawing a line above eyes ever darker.

When Rilke heard a voice from the cliff's edge at Castle Duino, who spoke back to him? Rilke had been begging and brooding for great inspiration. For some voice to come out of the darkness and guide his pen. He was searching for words worthy of existence. And then this voice:

Who, if I cried out, would hear me among the angelic
orders? Even if one of them pressed me to his heart
I'd be consumed in the force of his being. For beauty is
nothing
but the beginning of terror, and we are amazed when
it casually spares us.

With these words, he was given his path, brief moments of salvation. He had cried out to the divine world, to any god who could hear him, and it spoke back harshly that there is no one to turn to in human's time of need. Further pressing the separateness of human and *how little at home we are / in the interpreted world.*

Is this not magic? The acquisition of a greater truth that had to be pulled from grief, heard from the abyss. A prayer answered in the form of a voice in a poet's mind. Is this not insanity's twin? My mother said she has an altar where she holds together all of her special people. She says prayers for them every night. Her book of spells is just a way of understanding the mystery where she has always found herself. We are a family of poison and cure.

I have received two housewarming gifts here in the mountains: a broom and an axe. The broom, though useful, was a joke from one of my "witchy" friends. She said it was for good luck. Then she cackled and said *just in case you need a new ride home.* Myths and superstitions piling up like lumber in the woods after a flood. Spilling into narratives from my mind.

The axe was given to me to make use of the abundant resources of Appalachia. This land of wives' tales and folk heroes still boasts elements of survival and simplicity. People here burn wood because it is plentiful. They grow tomatoes and potatoes, snap peas and apples because the land will hold their roots. These densely green hills are home to ancient trees balancing the oxygen, sheltering chipmunks and birds, shading the grasshoppers and spiders, leaving behind twigs and branches for winter's fire, providing perch for the crane, should one pass through. These living creatures of self-sustaining energy laying down ring after ring. I run my hand along a cedar and can almost hear it sing.

Poisons are reminders of why we live. How we can be so daring as to try to live well. To call out to mystery and expect to hear a voice, to find a way out of illness, darkness, or insanity. To cure: to restore or preserve. To survive in connected existence.

As night draws nearer, the birds' whistles reduce to peeps, shallow stirrings from the nest drowned out by crickets insistent on being heard. Some of nature falls asleep, while the rest begin their wild night. This continuous cycle like a great wheel beyond where I perceive the sky interconnecting existence into one mighty illusion. That this life could ever be two. That we could ever be alone.

That an uprooted tree trunk can turn on its side and become a crane. That jewelweed's leaves turn silver in dew. That the willow can turn rain into golden mist. That what we fashion from our fascinations are our greatest hopes. That we may live in the manner of cranes: curious, attentive, crucial, and absolutely bewitched.

UNRAVELING IV

Words hold history, but the common terms of 2020 were still in the earliest stages of learning themselves. According to the Global Language Monitor, which tracked words in English across the world for 2020, the most used word of the year was "COVID-19," while *Time* magazine highlighted "Karen" as an important emerging word. "COVID" is short for "coronavirus" and was born in 2020. It was created from the roots: Corona + Virus + Disease. The coronavirus, some say, looks like the corona of the sun, so is rooted in Rome's crown or garland, given as an honor for military service—an aggressive name for a virus.

A Karen is a privileged white woman, but the name wasn't born in 2020. "Karen" was probably born in 2004 or 2005 in the movie *Mean Girls* or a comedy skit by Dane Cook who quipped that "there's a Karen in every group, and in every case she's always a bag of douche." The joke crescendos when Cook says that when "Karen" walks away everyone looks at each other and says, "God, Karen, she's such a douche-bag!" But Karen didn't officially take off until Memorial Day in 2020. On this day during a global panic, George Floyd would be murdered a few hours after Amy Cooper called the police on a man in Central Park. Amy Cooper's dog was wrongly off leash in the same area where Christian Cooper was birding. He asked her to please leash her dog. Instead of honoring his request, Amy Cooper called the police claiming her life was being threatened by an African American man. The video of their encounter, recorded by Christian Cooper, would go viral. Later, Cooper's sister Melody would tweet, *Oh, when Karens take a walk with their dogs off leash in the famous Bramble in NY's Central Park.*

Two ends of a thread pulled tight into a knot: COVID and Karen. The anchor lines were set long ago: as old as the invention of agriculture and the class system; as old as colonization and the fundamental changes in human consciousness that would occur. In an interview Christian Cooper said Amy Cooper is not the point. He explains that her claim led to a viral response because of a "deep vein of racial bias" in America.

Spiders attach more lines to their blueprint than they will use. From these attachments, all will be cut away except the seven primary lines. Biologist Jonathan A. Coddington writes *now that you have the seven attachments you need, you*

no longer need to touch the ground, leaves, twigs, anything , , , you are in your own, arguably solipsistic, world.

In *Caste: The Origins of Our Discontents*, Isabel Wilkerson metaphorically compares America to an old house on a piece of land. The deeper you look inside a house's bones, the deeper and more complex its history. Wilkerson encourages you to not ignore the basement, to enter the basement and not avoid what you would prefer not to see. She describes the land the house is on, so beautiful on the exterior, but underneath the gleam is unstable loam and rock, "heaving and contracting over generations." Arguably, European colonizers brought seven attachments to this land: genocide, gold, religion, whiskey, individualism, patriarchy, and a long history of a caste system—what Wilkerson defines as a construction, "a fixed and embedded ranking of human value that sets the presumed supremacy of one group against the presumed inferiority of other groups on the basis of ancestry and often immutable traits." A caste system is rigid, composed of boundaries and binaries. Thread these seven attachments with European diseases and we have the violent and systemic overthrow of a sophisticated continent of people and nations.

The spider then begins to spin its web. The silk is drawn out quickly, predictably—attached by tiny ravels between two attachments. The spider curates its web from the outside, working its way inward, concentrically, segment by segment.

I lost the ability to hug when quarantine started. Because of my frozen shoulders, hugs were more like a cat pressing against your legs. The physical therapist had me stretching five times each day and the acupuncturist heated what appeared to be antique glass light bulb covers and suctioned them to my skin. He would rub them up and down my shoulder and bicep until I cried out—it was like rubbing a stone over jagged diamond tips.

A local witch and healing practitioner in Seattle, Ylva, advised me to have a conversation with my burgundy pillow—the one bought for top surgery and now used again a few months later for frozen shoulder recovery. She suggested the pillow may be carrying the impression of a former gender expression and that the pillow may have something to share. She also said that my frozen joints suggest parts of me are displaced and that I need to partner with these places and speak with them. She also said I need to hold a funeral.

Then the spider starts to spin its web, a relatively simple and predictable process. It begins at the outside and works its way in, attaching segment by segment with its legs, creating concentric circles.

When I spoke with Ylva I could energetically sense all the knots in my body compete to rise forward. There was my old gender expression, my ongoing struggles regulating myself with my whiteness and complicity, the untouched reservoir of my ancestry, my broken mother and silent brother. There were hidden knots there, too—ones too hot to look at—too dangerous for the system of my life. I wasn't sure if the funeral should be a dumpster fire or patient ceremony with slow burning candles, and I wasn't sure what to throw into the fire.

On Senses: A Nature Essay

Since this is a nature essay, I should explain that while my body is located in an experimental forest, it is so far from its senses that all I smell is the sour pungency of a warm beer and the pitiful pool of wax at the bottom of a controlled flame near the air vent of my computer. Since I am here, and outside is there, I strain my ears to hear early dusk sweeping the landscape of its dust, settling early layers of dew on each sword of the sword fern which will sink imperceptibly lower to the ground as it gathers the burden of night, or the yellow grosbeak who fed well this day and spreads its shallow fibers in a low thicket while the beetles continue their work of gnawing tunnels and laying eggs for tomorrow's pileated woodpecker shrieking the forest awake. But that is outside.

Here, Johann Sebastian Bach makes shape with sound, isolates me, and somehow reminds me of *we*; that we die alone: *Et un Spiritum*; the bass vocalist speaks and plans, the music is the organized shape of linear progress. Then quandary, the unison of spiraling shapes, the de-centered self in communion with the divine. Finally solace and acceptance, the triumphant trumpet when we've let go of our need to know.

The shape is a billow of smoke, a plume that mushrooms then releases. You see him there, his conductor's baton whipping shapes in the air, the organic construction of imagination, the very essence of what it means to be.

This is representation summoning imagination, or is it? What can be said of the state of my being as the phonograph spins the record's lines toward completion, grooves of the nature of spirit until the needle's arm lifts and the silence of our endings shifts in a minute's static where my spirit writhes in my body, stepping out like a cloud just above the mountain ridge, or like a pocket of humid air in a sunlit meadow. Where am I to turn here, my spirit dancing above a rendered body laying down language like song?

I see metaphor here; that carved well of longing—we see our reflections, but can never touch its depths; and here on this page—the page that receives these letters, the one you translate now—the one that leaves me only the porous grief of disconnection where our spirits fall flat in our literal system of language—here we are left with metaphor for the longing of shared experience, the communal sounds of our imaginations that tell us we are not alone, yet these messages are the great heaving of emotion through tunnels of the unknown.

Here is an exercise in loneliness:

> Exercise 1: Imagine your mind in the shape of this sentence.
>
> Exercise 2: Now, this one: the hostility of our moon tonight holds the night sky hostage, a vestibule of confessions here on the ground below, a vestibule of stars in my heart—I await the darker hour of our being.

But wait, this is a nature essay, right? The world out there. I should tell you about the hummingbird outside my window. The sides of its neck in a crimson stole, cedar green body coating its heartbeat which seems the center point of gravity for its upright, astute posture. I should have described the wings' sound for you, tricking you into making shapes with your mind by appealing to your senses. Daring you to consider what it means to be by placing you under its wing.

To try, this essay's shape a near-blind hummingbird zipping from leaf to leaf in search of a bloom's sugar, that first sip when the sun shifts from shadow to light and the fuchsia glows, a trumpet of survival. Go there, too, inside the trumpet where the sugar is a translucent bead, a pearl for another, a life.

If it pleases, imaginatively cut and paste the hummingbird section just before the Bach section. Trust in the shape of nature's image, then follow the thread to Bach. This is a Choose Your Own Adventure in the imagination of your mind and body. This essay is for you, and I trust your translation implicitly.

Or try this: The essay is warm and I hike the steep, narrow path toward its southern ridge. The forest is called experimental because it has been restored, and I hear the shape of my own being in there.

To restore is to return to a natural state, or to return to innocence. It's a way of saying, you were perfect the first time, let's get back to that—it is un-creating through creation; it is healing.

This essay is Pacific Northwest mud. You know this mud, you've sunk there and wanted to stay, but pulled your foot from the earth instead. Near the essay's summit a sudden vibration recalled the flap of hummingbird wings, cold and small, then the sound grew warmer, took on the hot breath of a mammal—a purr, a growl—a very large cat. I can't explain the sound, the essay fails here. *You know: the growl of a large cat.* But no, you can't hear that. The cool vibration in its throat was a pair of fast wings. We are getting there: come with me—the growl was warm fur in the sun, a watery purr with teeth, the sound of wild grinding its teeth against the edge of a species that rendered time into an unforgiving clock of loss.

And there it is. Loss. It was a cougar.

We dedicate our lives to letters but realize their failure in a time of historic extinction. I am inside but my words are outside. You are inside, too, and I put you outside by challenging your senses. That cougar was one of the last of its kind, there is no mate in the wild that we have left for her, no magical den constructed of language for her to hide within. In nature's wild you seek what you need, but in our constructed wild you avoid what you hope not to find. In this room I seek wildness through a glass window that opens by a crank; the air is cold but I breathe it in, past my lungs to where my gut clenches my will and cleaves me to a body that I barely know is mine. In my wild, I run from the cougar, its breath hot on my back.

RESTORATION OF WOLVES

Gusts of wind drove through Wyoming's turgid valleys shaking the truck we slept in. All I could think of were the cracks in the local roads paved above glaciers from the Ice Age. How the road had to be repaved each year. I thought about the lava's heat underneath the glaciers melting the ice, but mostly I wanted to smell the past in those cracks. Ancient ice and lava, their minerals and bones the foundations of planetary systems—there's spirit there—and I was falling asleep above its lungs. C was already asleep, stretched out as much as they could in a seat that couldn't recline, a crown of steam gathered on the window. It was about to be opening night at the Slough Creek Campground in Lamar Valley, an area famous for wildlife viewing—though the major attraction was wolves.

We had pulled into the campground's parking lot around 5 P.M. when the sun was still generous, stretching the valley's bowl east to west. There were already a few campers here, and C had hoped that if we gave the guys next to us a chocolate bar that they'd tell us how to get a campsite. I was cynical of those guys, but I am always doubtful of *those guys*. The internet had given us conflicting information: campground opens at 9 A.M., campground may open at 6 A.M., arrive by 6 A.M., arrive the night before, avoid getting fined for parking overnight, you'll need to park overnight. We arrived determined, and C—Jersey-Italian and a magnet for people—did the talking for us.

Down one chocolate bar and with scarce information, a park ranger arrived. She told us we had to leave by sundown, but there was a message between the lines that she was also trying to give. *If* I come back, I'll ticket you. There was a sparkly glimmer on *if*, and we decided to bank on it.

I brought us to the Lamar Valley because I wanted to know how it felt to walk where wolves walk, to sleep where they hunt, to have the wind carry their howls down the cliffs. Not the memory of the species, nor the wandering lone wolf looking for an extinct mate. I guess I wanted to believe in something more, if only for a few days. I think I was lonely.

This was also our second anniversary trip—two years since our wedding ceremony in North Carolina when C wrote vows about a math equation for attraction; two years since we fused with the landscape in the Airstream nestled into the Sierra Nevadas; two years since the measurements started. In that time the measurements grew in subtle ways, though I learned to measure our love as depth as well as distance, making the configurations of loneliness much more complex.

This was our plan: to combine literary wolf research with relationship reconnection.

This was our plan: slowly drive a rental car from Seattle to Yellowstone, conclude how to get a campsite for the week at the popular campground at Slough Creek, pitch a tent upon volcanic ground and hope it turns out okay, cook delicious foods that won't hurt our stomachs too much, and discover why wolves are famous in Yellowstone.

We left the campground parking lot when the ranger asked us to, then went to our hotel room to sleep until 3 A.M., at which time we returned to Slough Creek. Our headlights pushed away the wilderness that had crept in overnight. Humans were tucked away in their containers, and now it was owl's time, the cool hours for hunting and herding. The unfamiliar sagebrush looked like ghost's fingers in the gray light of our high beams. C reminded me to take my time while I sipped on watery instant coffee from the hotel.

At the campground, three campers were already lined up at the gate. I pulled in behind them, wondering who they were, what they came here for. I wondered if opening night was always such a dramatic exhibition, if someone might come by offering hors d'oeuvres on tiny toothpicks. But instead, a new stillness, a new darkness, the wind clearing the valley of what didn't belong there anymore.

In 1995, gray wolves were reintroduced to Yellowstone National Park. Fourteen wolves from several packs in Canada were tracked, stunned, contained, and transported to several regions in the park—including Lamar Valley. To animal biologists, this was a necessary and logical decision: elk in the park were abundant because the top predators who hadn't been extirpated—grizzly bears and coyotes—weren't adept at hunting them. Deer populations had swollen, and the ecology of the park was showing signs of the imbalance. To animal biologists, this was also a necessary ethical decision: Doug Smith, the leading biologist and wolf expert, referred to it as "lifting a burden." The gray wolf and red wolf are indigenous to North America from current day Canada to Mexico. When colonizers from Europe arrived there were as many as half a million to a million wolves. But in just a few centuries they cleared the way for European expansion by eliminating the wolf from the landscape. As early as the 1880s, very few wolves were left in the country. The last wolf killed in Yellowstone was in 1936.

What's important to note here is how recent this history is. America's history is very young and is designed to forget itself. The settler colonial plan for the wolf: make it extinct. This was an especially deliberate extinction legislated by the US government. Even Theodore Roosevelt, lauded naturalist, beloved by many nature writers, called wolves "the beast of waste and destruction," and supported the ruthless end of its species.

Yes, history is young: hunters were still wandering around the forests of northern Michigan and Minnesota in the 1970s hoping to kill one of the few remaining wolves. Also, in the 1970s, the gray wolf was added as an endangered animal to the newly inked Endangered Species Act (ESA). This represented a very late wake-up in the revision of America since the species was nearly rendered extinct. But history continued to unfold: the gray wolf in Wyoming was de-listed from the ESA in 2014. In the same year in Idaho, to sarcastically celebrate the fortieth anniversary of the ESA, hunters proposed a two-day contest to reward whoever could kill the most wolves and coyotes, while trappers were sent to kill each member of the wolf packs who lived in remote areas of the Frank Church River of No Return Wilderness. Indeed, America's young history—between wolves and colonial America—is still unfolding.

I stared at the moonlight along the dashboard there in the Lamar Valley—former home of the Druid Peak pack, one of the largest recorded packs ever, with thirty-seven members. The Lamar Canyon pack is somewhere outside these windows and is in disarray. And this chaos is the result of how I came to know of the charismatic and most photographed wild wolf in the country, 832F, who had been killed just a few years before.

Sunrise gradually revealed the valley to us, and the wind died down to a hush. The cliffs of Druid Peak were brief outlines below a stunned yellow sky. We both woke up when the camper in front of us started its engine, a thick funnel of smoke releasing from its tailpipe. "Should we go out there?" C asked, looking around us to be sure our place in line was secure. The line of cars moved one by one, so I began to practice in my head what to ask the park ranger. C prompted me with more questions, I practiced mine—it felt like so much was on the line in that moment. We pulled up and the park ranger smiled at us knowingly; she seemed proud of us for being fourth in line—she made us feel like we worked hard, did it right, and belonged there. She suggested several campsites that were the "best," so we chose the one nearest a game trail—a crossing path for animals to get to the creek. We were on the edge of the animals' wilderness.

We both wanted to have a ceremony for our union, but neither of us knew if we believed in marriage. The word reeked of heteronormativity, of disaster. Does marriage make sense for queer people? How much change can partnership hold? We decided to write our own agreements and plan a ceremony that felt like a community understanding of our love; we wanted everyone there to know what we meant by partnership, though I'm not certain that we knew exactly what that meant, except that we didn't want to erase ourselves for each other.

Our ceremony in North Carolina was the greatest moment of feeling loved as adults. We felt high from being seen, for being celebrated, being embraced. We were too exhausted to make love that night, instead we made a tight knot with our bodies in the king-sized bed.

Ours was the only tent in the campsite. Everyone else brought pop-up trailers or campers. Their containers looked sealed, sturdy, and frankly luxurious. We pitched our two-person tent tightly in the earth, remembering the wind from the night before. Our canopy offered shade and we hid our food in the bear-proof locker. After breakfast, there was a stir from the older couple next to us. A shout. A point to the meadow. A black bear.

She had her nose trained on a pile of ant larvae about twenty-feet from our tent. We looked at each other with our best "Oh shit" look, then jumped in the truck. The bear's body was an amazing heap of fur and power, though her grace at scooping the larvae was soft as moonlight. She sniffed around and moved on but left an impression. We understood why people came here in campers rather than tiny tents.

In 1872 Yellowstone became a national park, protecting 2.2 million acres for their awe-inspiring composition of mountains, valleys, canyons, geysers, hot springs, and wildlife. The park was intended as a "pleasuring ground for the benefit and enjoyment of the people." Yes, *pleasuring* as a verb. In 1895, more than five thousand visitors entered the park pleasuring. I don't have photographs, but I am certain that the pleasurers were semi-affluent and white.

Today, almost five million people come here to pleasure themselves each year.

I don't like public pleasuring. I feel too queer, too on the edge of an unknown gender; my pleasuring doesn't fit in with mainstream pleasuring—excepting a few movies and the occasional music show. My time in the world outside of queer and artist communities is spent on its edges; fully alive alone in a field, deeply recoiled when someone calls me “lady” or acknowledges me as a woman. People see C and I hold hands sweetly and they recoil. There’s a lot of recoiling around us.

Yet, both C and I are deeply sensitive and loving: we love pleasure.

Slough Creek Campground seemed almost perfect; away from the five million people, sunny, nestled near a creek. The challenges were the constancy of people milling around campers, refreshing their daylong relationship with Bud Light, and swinging binoculars from tree to tree. It was sweet-natured, but there was a spotlight. I washed behind our small tent, ducking behind it to change my underwear.

We stayed in a private Airstream on a cliffside in the Sierra Nevadas for our honeymoon. A dog named Piha checked on us each day, wagging her tail next to eggs delivered to us earlier. Next to the trailer was an outdoor kitchen and a bathhouse. The cast-iron tub was so spacious we could both stretch out. It held the water’s heat for hours. On the first night we lit each tea light and melted into the water, melted into the landscape. It all just melted away: our move to Seattle, my insecurities, their depression and anxiety, money, capitalism, environmental violence, racism, queer identities: gone. We did not feel lonely.

We returned to each other, too; a reintroduction. We were lovers again for those few days. C said the moment was like an opening that we moved into. I remember it as moving into a portal of time and energy that was restorative, open, and bright.

Our campsite secure, we packed water and our favorite Cliff bars and headed out of the valley to search for a wolf. Or to search for others searching for a wolf. Or to determine the reason for searching for something that is supposed to be wild.

An introduction suggests making the way for something, an opening to bring something in; it is context—a moment of looking into another's eyes before you begin to know them informally. I don't remember being formally introduced to C; sometimes you glimpse someone's spirit first. I remember the performance of a fiction piece in graduate school that I thought was almost poetry. I have no idea what it was about, but it was piercing and complex. We talked in the hall afterwards, and I appreciated how the other students melted away. I thought that maybe we shared a depth and a privacy; that we shared a way of being in the world.

Wolves handle introductions a little differently. For them it is a way of being *with* the world. In a video we see a dark gray male wolf who has strayed from the Rose Creek pack. He wants to mate; he's looking for a new pack to join. He calls to the Druid Peak pack, a complicated and questioning howl. The Druids howl back, but the deep tone of their alpha male, #38, is missing.

When the male wolf meets the pack, the introduction—the preliminary opening—is tense. The line between death and belonging is both fragile and terse. The pack smells him, tests him—they are reading his nerve and his will. At first, he responds and stands his ground. Then he makes himself a statue under their threat. He can take it. After several hours of testing, he is accepted into the pack. The joy of community and belonging—the playfulness of a secure future for the pack—creates an opening we'd all be lucky to experience.

Wolves did not require a formal introduction to this land; they evolved and adapted here. In fact, the ecology of Yellowstone has been shaped by the patterns wolves and other animals have created for millions of years. The story of their reintroduction is not a story at all—or shouldn't be. It is what would naturally happen. But since a plane had to fly them over human-controlled lands to get here, since biologists had to adapt them to the landscape for several weeks so they wouldn't run off looking for Canada, since they had to exist within an invisible boundary so humans didn't kill them—we have a story.

Here's the amazing thing about Yellowstone: there are nonhuman animals everywhere.

Here's the problematic thing about Yellowstone: there are humans clumped up everywhere on the roadsides staring at them; slamming their brakes on the highway because something somewhere moved; leaning from their windows with cameras shoved into bisons' faces, approaching bison calves in flip flops and collared shirts.

If I were to paint a portrait of human loneliness, I'd have taken out a canvas and done a plein air composition of a traffic jam caused by bison crossing some road built on top of a melting glacier and some guy approaching them wearing a culturally appropriated flowered shirt and khakis.

We had received a packet of information when we entered the park, including a yellow flyer that depicted a male tourist who had been gored and vaulted into the air by a bison. His camera and ball cap flew up; the camera pointed at him. The caption read WILD ANIMALS ARE DANGEROUS. The flyer went on to say why they are dangerous and how to behave around them. It suggested that all pleasuring should occur inside your car. It said that tents "are not secure."

We took our time on that first day, scoping out hikes and getting our bearings. The bears had their bearings; we did not. Sunrise and sunset were the suggested times to go looking for wolves, so after dinner we drove to a densely populated lookout along the highway. At first, we loitered around. C looked for someone who I should meet so I could get more information on finding a wolf. I avoided people who wanted to talk about wolves. I was role playing, halfheartedly trying to be a good environmental literary journalist: I wore my binoculars, scanning the hills for movement; I sat near other folks doing the same thing and eavesdropped; I tried to find the remnants of a carcass that a guy with a spotting scope told us about, but couldn't see anything. I was feeling more like a poet—one who stands on the edges of existence. One who, if I stayed there long enough, might realize something about being alive.

C asked if I wanted to get away from all the people, and I did. We were both not pleasuring. We knew we didn't belong there. We spotted a skinny trail through a meadow that wound back toward the hill just below where the spotting scopes were pointed. There were a few bison near its base. It felt good to be away from the other spectators. There must have been forty cars of people, and several couples appeared to be tailgating: beers in koozies, chips, pretzels, hot dogs, mini grills. It was like a football game was about to begin, and the teams were Wolf vs. Elk—a Wildlife Superbowl match.

We were nervous on the walk: this was not a place for wandering humans. I mean, it was: it was a trail created for human feet as well as nonhuman paws and hooves. But this is where animals hunt and poop and fight and eat and sleep. Not a place for us. Yet as we walked, I felt myself unwind toward the animal world. I felt the activity of tracking, my nose sharper, the awareness of my own nervous odor. The path was muddy, and we spotted the impression of a wolf paw. My heart knelt into it.

We didn't "see" anything except for all the amazing things we saw. We would learn over our week at Yellowstone the constancy of "Did you see?" and "Is there anything to see here?" It would feel like we were burning Annie Dillard's essay "Seeing" repeatedly. Back in the parking lot a Spanish-speaking family was looking for something and the children seemed bored. One of the kids approached us and said, "Did you see the wolf that was shadowing you along the path?" I said no. She said her mom watched a wolf follow us along the path. I looked to her and she saw somehow into me.

The rest of the week was characterized by general discomfort and a lack of pleasuring. We slept separated by the cold and wind, mildly panicked of becoming food for a grizzly. One night I woke up to a significant sniffing just outside our tent. I didn't wake C—they already had their fill of anxiety. We went to shower once at a less primitive campsite, but one look at the shower room filled with beach towels and hair dryers told me we didn't belong there. In the sea of red USA shirts and Coronas, I felt like the first genderqueer person these people had ever seen. The looks were long, trailing me. We started down one hiking trail only to be warned off by a "recent carcass" flyer. Down the next trail a male pronghorn squared his shoulders and chased us back. On another trail, the giant claws of a grizzly had scratched a section of a tree away. The wilderness was keeping us out, as if a flyer had been handed to the animals: HUMAN ANIMALS ARE DANGEROUS.

Queer people reckon with safety every day. I was visibly transmasculine then and C was femme in appearance but with a complicated gender. Every time we walk through a door, we seem to force our existences into a new room. Some rooms are too unsafe to enter. On our drive through Idaho C had to pay for gas while I stayed in the car—it wasn't safe for me in there.

I have always found safety and belonging in the animal world. Not because animals want me around, but because they don't gender me. There are no social rules that have been constructed by animals to exclude me. So, in a way, the Coronas and beach towels were a greater threat to me than the fresh piles of scat the size of watermelons. We spent the week negotiating safe spaces, finding peace for only brief moments.

The morning we did see a wolf was the last time we'd go looking for one. Our campsite was populated almost exclusively by animal biologists and naturalists. The couple next to us, John and Betty, were friends with the lead wolf trackers in the park who'd synchronized their radio signal with the signal of the rangers—they were who you followed for a sighting. They rushed to their truck and said, "Follow us if you want to see a wolf!" At that point, we didn't want to, but C reminded me that this was why we were here—so we hurried. We followed the dry dust kicked up by their truck to the highway, where we saw a huge clump of people. Binoculars, spotting scopes: we were all there to see something. To really see it.

And we did. A tiny speck in the meadow sitting behind sage brush. Through my binoculars I saw the ginger-colored wolf's handsome ears revolving through our sounds: the gasping, oohing, tracking sounds of our modern species. I reluctantly spoke to a park ranger. I asked him about wolf 832F, the "Famous Wolf of Yellowstone" who was killed in the winter of 2012. The wolf from the *New York Times* article. He couldn't recall her. Maybe he remembers something about a she alpha who was killed. Not sure. She wasn't famous to him at all.

I asked him why someone might describe a wolf as famous or as a "rock star," and he wondered about the connection between people seeing their own wild nature in the eyes of wolves. He said, "You begin to see them, and it sticks: you want the chase, you want to see."

After the wolf trotted off, the carnival of spectators milled around looking lost: nothing to see here. Cheryl and Dave's radio clicked out a fuzzy voice. In a panic they grabbed their gear and sprinted to their van. The human clumps rushed to follow. They were off to go find themselves in another wolf.

In my journal I wrote, *Stun me, collar me, test me—I disappear by retreat.*

In December of 2012 C clipped an article for me: "'Famous' Wolf Is Killed Outside Yellowstone." It told the story of 832F, the alpha female of the Lamar Valley pack. She had wandered past the invisible park boundary and was shot. Her brother was killed nearby just a few weeks earlier.

I researched 832F, trying to identify the conditions of her fame. Articles talked about her visibility to humans, how she would seem to entertain them rather than shy away. They tried to imagine how many photographs of her existed around the globe. They labeled her a worldwide sensation. Yet the park ranger saw her as just another wolf.

What hungriness within the human species does fame fulfill? Fame was not the state of being of that wolf—her fame was a story constructed from the millions of visitors who came looking for wildness. They shared a question: What is it like to be her, roaming these cliffs, managing her pack, accelerating toward an exhausted elk, seizing her fangs into its throat? 832F was the reflection of a pervasive loneliness among us: the distance between our selves and our experiences—our animal bodies restless while our minds stare at illuminated screens.

After a hike up Specimen Ridge in which we sang Meatloaf and Whitney Houston songs to alert bears of our presences, passed by elk horn sculptures, and stepped over immense bear poop piles, we finally gave in to secure tourism in our vehicle. We drove to the fog in Hayden's Valley that kept the people away, drove to some geysers where the instability of the ground shook our spirits, and spent time in an air-conditioned gift store. We purchased a roll of Sweet Sixteen chocolate donuts because a woman who admires the red fox at our campground ate them each morning. These are the travels of people who love each other, but don't touch in the night; whose bodies need the wildness of this place but don't know how to open to it. C said, "All the animals have a job except for us. We are just walking aimlessly."

In the restoration of wolves to Yellowstone, something of our human spirit is trying to heal. The empty spaces within us are far from pretty, and I continue to calculate the cost on our planet. The frantic search for feeling alive through unembodied experiences is a gruesome spectacle, one that the animals of the park contend with daily through the lenses of binoculars and cameras. I wonder if we should finally say *enough*; if the park should close to pleasuring humans.

On our final night we retreated to Trout Lake—a place people do not gather to view wildlife or seek the restoration of wolves. It was wind-quiet as the blues of dusk settled upon us. Two ravens flew immediately overhead; the sun lowered behind the mountain. A wolf let go of a howl that nearly returned us.

UNRAVELING V

Ice tells a story of the planet through bubbles, ash, density. An orthographical study read week by week through the slow crushing of ice layer by layer—another version of the newspaper. Tree resin holds the narrative of insects and flowers, primitive birds and lizards. Recently, part of a three-dimensional dinosaur was discovered in the ninety-nine-million-year-old time capsule of resin and amber—see it there: partial wing in an arc, skull, neck; the splay of tiny talons. Frozen in time.

Here is the story the pillow told me of my body:

Your right shoulder is composed of hatchets and axes hammering into steel. The steel is a kind of machinery held together by your evasiveness. The secret is your tenderness. You learned to hide this because you had no protection. You learned to seize, freeze.

Years ago, I found a picture of myself at six months old. My jaw perfectly center under puffy baby cheeks, my mouth a silly, round, gaping O. Eyes so bright. I walked to the bathroom mirror and tried at least twenty smiles, but none matched the openness in the photograph. The left side of my jaw was set, the right side locked to the right. It looked like my jaw was going two ways at once, straining my smiles into half-hearted sorrow. I made a commitment to find that smile.

I wonder what story ice would tell us of 2020? What planetary evolution or revolution would be layered in ice if climate change wasn't melting ice faster than it can settle? Where would COVID and Karen, Pandemic and Loneliness, nestle in its memory? In this age of historic ice melt, we are left to read the past as quickly as possible before its memory is washed away.

Merriam-Webster recently updated *doomscrolling* from a word to watch to a word in its dictionary. This comes just four years after adding the singular "they" to its tome. Doomscrolling is its own pandemic whose consequence is catastrophically isolating. It is a negative cycle of learning and behavior that defines the world as dangerous and apocalyptic, generally forcing the doomscroller into a seizure of the nervous system: fight, flight, freeze. I love to read the headlines on DemocracyNow.org, imagining the trustworthy voice of Amy Goodman delivering the headlines. But here is a list of today's headlines:

Blinken Meets with Netanyahu as Israel Kills Scores of More Palestinians in Gaza

Displaced Palestinians Blast Blinken for Helping "Israel Kill Children"

Video Shows Israeli Military Vehicle Driving Over Palestinian Man Shot Dead in West Bank

Israeli Lawmaker Faces Possible Expulsion for Supporting South Africa's Genocide Case Against Israel

Jeremy Corbyn Urges Britain to Back Genocide Case Against Israel

Israel Strikes Lebanon Again; U.S. Officials Concerned Netanyahu Sees Broader War Is Key to "His Political Survival"

Pro-Ceasefire Protesters Disrupt Biden Speech at Church in Charleston, SC

325 Arrested for Shutting Down Bridges and Tunnel in Manhattan Calling for Gaza Ceasefire

Workers at Key Boeing Subcontractor Had Warned About "Excessive Amount of Defects" in Plane Products

Trump Claims Presidential Immunity Should Shield Him from Charges Tied to 2020 Election

> Pro-Democracy Rallies Held in Brazil One Year After Jan. 8 Insurrection
>
> Scientists Confirm 2023 Was Hottest Year on Record
>
> Fire Leaves over 7,000 Rohingya Refugees Homeless in Bangladesh
>
> Asylum Seekers from India on Hunger Strike at Northwest Detention Center

How is your body? Your breathing?

Can you take in the final headline, that last step in the pattern of colonial doom?

GRAMMAR OF GENDER

The day I was discovered as a girl who might not be a girl I rustled alone in a sleeping bag in my neighbor's front yard counting leaf shadows on the tent's evening surface. The young maple leaves outside were distinct from their shadows then as I watched near-black shapes ebb into each other's spaces. I watched the layering of shade like a child watches clouds pass. I waited for the shadows to separate so I could contain each with a number: 16, 17, 18. I wanted to get the number right before the sun squeezed below the trees in the woods rounding my neighborhood. I wanted to get the number right so I could fall asleep.

What is your son's name? the cosmetics counter woman would say. They all said this. My mother shopped almost daily, and they all knew her: Lancôme, Chanel, Estee Lauder—the ladies behind counters. No matter the woman's name she would unclasp the plastic eyeshadow box that was the shape of a shell. She would lift the tiny brush from its cradle and swipe its satin swab into a circle of sparkling color. She would apply a stripe onto my mother's hand. Then another. A palette would appear like a sunset; a new person; the spring collection.

The shell is a home for women like my mother. Once you know the language of behavior—a delicate balance of paranoia and comfort; a piercing tightness in the eyes—you can spot those for whom shopping is an addiction. Those whose obsessions with appearance are crookedly folded into them. I think of Gaston Bachelard's metaphor of the shell as a home, a motionless place to hide, and "by staying in the motionlessness of its shell, the creature is preparing temporal explosions, not to say whirlwinds, of being." So, the shell is one way to contain oneself in an unmovable space to eventually find a way out—a new way of being.

Yet I wonder at the implications of this for my mother, haunted by voices, altered realities, and uncontrollable moods. If mental illness is her shell, it has been a shell for life—and those temporal explosions her everyday fight for control. Gold, rose, green. *Click*, went the shell. And what followed was a world of color.

The cosmetic ladies' words made me feel sparkly, like I was getting away with a special trick. My mom would smirk—half embarrassed, half charmed—and say that I am her daughter. Everyone would blush a little, then I'd pull my Red Sox cap down over my eyes and smile. *Click.*

I could hear my friends still running around outside, the grassy lawn absorbing their noise. We were having a neighborhood sleepover, separate tents for boys and girls. We were in the fifth grade, and my friend Lisa Anderson, who I didn't really like, was the first girl in my class to develop breasts and hips. Her body seemed older than mine and this gave her power. I had almost-breasts, near-breasts, tiny painful domes that I wished away every night when I lay in bed counting shadows. We all lived on Fort Devens, an Army base in Massachusetts that woke up to the sound of cannon fire at dawn. The cannon would sound, and soldiers would stop jogging or pull their cars to the side of the road, locate the nearest American flag, and stand in salute. This was the last year that I'd have close friends and childhood crushes. The last year in which recess was a time for imagination. The last year of racial innocence between friends, when my friend Katrinka and I would spend the summer playing games in the yard while our parents looked on with worry.

The flap to the tent door was unzipped and in the near-dark I heard a foot catch the door's lip. A noisy breath was quickly on top of me, then a sudden pressure on my breast. I only remember the pain of being grabbed, searched, and the sound of breath so close I felt its heat. He got up and ran out yelling *She doesn't have boobs, there's no titties!* The voice belonged to Victor, the kid next door who could never catch me at recess. Everyone laughed. I lay so still in the sleeping bag that I literally changed the shape of my body into a stillness—a clamp. I had been searched and revealed; I was a girl—yet the facts of that were in question. And my body as an object for violence was made a keen possibility. *Click.*

We lay motionless in a shell "preparing temporal explosions . . . of being." *Temporal* refers to material existence or existence within time, so to prepare a temporal explosion is to prepare for an action—an action of being. But what action is suitable in the unsafe shell of the body? The spirit curled in there.

I will always remember my mother's hands with the ghostly stains of lipstick, the rubbed-down lines of eyeliner and the smeared sparkles of eye shadow. I learned color from her hands, the relationality of gray tones with lilacs and tans. I memorized a hundred shades of rose under the white lights of the cosmetic counter. I knew the female models in the posters by heart and could tell you the name of any fragrance and the shape of its bottle. When Liz Taylor introduced her perfume "Poison," I would fondle the bottle like a magic potion, careful not to spray the noxious smell inside. *Does this smell good on me*, my mom would always ask. She knew I'd say yes.

I like thinking of words in terms of tracing paper: you trace over an image, then put a new sheet down and trace; new sheet, a new trace, over and over again until you have the portrait of a word in time. I like this process of construction and deconstruction because the original word holds the value of its time. Seven centuries of tracing its image and you see the creation of its distorted meaning. *Click.*

In English language *gender* has two roots from two languages and borrows from another: first it signified a kind or sort; then it referred to sex, then race, then mankind. The *humain genre* of mankind in the twelfth century signified a "kind" of human. A century later gender took on grammatical significance, insisting upon a class of nouns and pronouns, a grammatical gender. And it was within this time of sorting humans into types when, in Western Europe, witchcraft—an ancient system of belief founded upon a genderless goddess—was declared a heretical act and the genocide of women and queer/trans bodies would imprint a permanent mark of violence upon these bodies.

In *The Spiral Dance*, Starhawk—a contemporary witch—describes the effects of *Malleus Malleficarum*—The Hammer of the Witches—a Catholic-driven treatise on the persecution of women and witchcraft published in 1486. The document details the sin of carnal lust, how women are susceptible to witchcraft because of their weakened genders and how evil is passed down from women to their children. The document resulted in three centuries of aggressive violence against women. Up to a hundred thousand witches were murdered in this "sorting" of people.

In the tradition of witchcraft gender is not an exclusive binary—in fact its creation story begins with a "complete" being whose name cannot be spoken. She floats in the darkness, then sees her reflection, her own light, in the curved mirror of space. She falls in love with it, by drawing it toward her using her inner power, essentially making love to herself. In this act a song was created, the song became waves, and from this motion came the world. Starhawk is careful to note that the feminine "her" invoked is not because the "complete being" was gendered, but simply to resist the systemic clout of belief in male gods. It's a play on words.

After I was discovered as a girl—one whose gender was in question—here is how I coped for the next twenty years:

On the outside, I tried various forms of camouflage:

banana clips; flipped '80s bangs; rolled jeans and high tops; wearing only black and white; speaking in two to three word replies; sharing through shrugs; playing sports alone; earning good grades; working full time; hiding in my room; masturbating to images of a man and a woman without knowing which person I was; hiding in the woods; medium-length hair; feminine-sort-of-androgynous clothes that may or may not have included lace; slumped shoulders; shallow breath; eye shadow

At thirty-three years old, I'd had one romantic fling that lasted for a total of five hours over two days. *Click*.

Words die when they are no longer used, or when no one is left to use them. They decay like the body in compost, but what do they add to the soil? What can grow from such a thing that lives in the mind or on the lip, or on paper or a computer chip? Virginia Woolf suggested that after one dies, "the words become disinfected, purified of the accidents of the living body." Words are alive in a sense, accruing meaning over time—the meanings given to them by the body; by each of us, "living out and about on people's lips." (Woolf's essay, "Craftsmanship" delivered in her own voice, is available in a BBC broadcast radio recording from April 29, 1937, on YouTube.)

At the Korean spa below the oldest lesbian bar in Seattle I felt my body and spirit slide together. The moment was tender, I curled into it. The spa is small: one soaking tub, a sauna, a steam room, and two slender pallets for resting. I was resting on a pallet, my body naked and warm from the soaking tub. I marveled: to feel alive for this very moment.

I thought about one of the few French phrases I remember from high school, *je suis*. I felt lost in the phrase, dipping deep into the water of that wē valley in the word. I am. I'd learned at this point that my partner at the time, C, had been struggling with suicide ideation for years. And so many of my college students felt these same hidden thoughts on a reel in their minds. *Je suis, I am, suicide*—a cycling teeter-totter in my mind. I wondered if suicide was rooted in being; a sickness in being, and how much of my own life had been a slow sickness in being. Not a killing, but a sick spirit tightly stored away.

Woolf goes on to argue that when using an old tool such as the English language, rather than creating new words it is the writer's job to "creat[e] new patterns with old tools. How can we combine the old words in new orders so that they survive, so that they create beauty, so that they tell the truth?" Her suggestion is that if we could do this—if any of us could do this—then "everything we would read would tell the truth." She was speaking as a critic of twentieth-century literature in the mid-1900s, but I also wonder if she was speaking as a queer person in a time in which a new wave of traditional values was sweeping many cultures around the planet. I wonder if she was seeing the same old words in the same old orders and not finding herself there.

In English, there are at least three categories of pronouns: traditional pronouns, conventions based on traditional pronouns, and nonconventional pronouns.

Traditional singular pronouns are *he*, *she*, and *one*. At different times in the evolution of the English language *he* and *one* both signified any universal person, though both uses are now quite dated.

Conventions based on traditional pronouns include singular *they*, *she/he*, *s/he*, and apostrophe (*h'/h'self*).

Nonconventional pronouns, which began to bloom in the 1970s and are an ever-evolving list of words, include *ze*, *zhe*, *xe*, *ve*, humanist (*hu*), Elverson (*eirself*), *jee*, *peh*, *per*, *ney*, Spivak (*emself*), *co*, *na*, *et*, *phe*, *heshe*, and many others. Each pronoun has a base ("ze") and forms that correspond to the demands of grammar ("mer," "zer," "zers," "zimself").

How does one find oneself among this list?
How does ze find zimself among this list?'
How do they find themselves among this list?
How does hu find humself among this list?
How does s/he find him/herself among this list?

When each of these young words dies, does the bearer of that word also die? What will last, and which is saying the truth? The memory of these young words—their echoes—are faint, except in those who bore them and their inexplicable connection to traditional pronouns—to the sorting of humans. "Words belong to each other," whispers Woolf.

How are we to survive the structure of grammatical institutions that ties new words to old patterns? I recently took on the pronoun *they*, but didn't want it at first. I don't identify as a they; or a he; or a she; or a ze. I have no relationship to those words. I hear only their echoes of objectivism and feel my body tighten each time I am forced to exist in another's sentence.

Old words + new patterns = truth.

"We do not allow words their anonymity," Woolf insists—and this is the key thesis to her impressions about the living nature of words. Words are alive, just as I am alive—and you. Since "words are alive, they do not have boundaries; they mesh, intertwine, gain dimension; they do not bind to our human boundaries. Words are inherently integrated with change." The human mind pins words down to single meanings. The human mind makes meanings. The human mind insists upon systems of living rather than life itself—a grammar of being alive.

Words are alive, they are based upon change. Rather than define, they grow as we grow. At the end of a student poetry reading, a dear student, Zak, addressed me as "they" in front of the audience. They thanked me for caring about them, for taking the time to see them. As Zak said "they," they looked at me pointedly, and tenderly. There was room in the word. I grew into it.

There is a part of my spirit still in that tent in Massachusetts, though the neighborhood was demolished after Fort Devens was decommissioned. What is left are the trees I climbed, the semicircle of Poplar Street, and the woods flanking either side of what used to be my home. I once walked to where the windows would be and looked inside. My mother was there making dinner, flipping through a beauty magazine with her nails done. As an Army brat, it never occurred to me to think about Victor again. Once a military family moves, they move on. But between our houses plants repair the disturbed land: Asiatic bittersweet, bindweed, Canada thistle, clover, green foxtail, ragweed. I plunge my hands into the prickly leaves, groping for a stem. My spirit bristles and fills. But the pattern created when Victor searched my chest is a fracture that has echoed each day since. I lay there and counted leaf patterns. I now read a poem and count metrical patterns. Yet I also remember how words call for each other, how they breathe for each other in an ecosystem of animacy. The root of *grammar* is Old French, *gramaire*. It is said that in the Middle Ages, those of the learned class studied *gramaire*, and that part of this knowledge was the study of magic. Old words in new patterns.

Once, in a drawing class my instructor guided us to stop drawing the figure. Instead, she said, you find the anchor of its spirit, then echo your marks outward. You find the spirit; you don't make it.

My spirit doesn't care about the body; it has no relationship to gender; only being. But under the human gaze I shrink and dissolve: *she*; what *she* said; *her* classes; *her* writing. The constant gaze and assignment feels like dying over and over. So maybe if I don't have breasts. Maybe if I can take back Victor's discovery of my body. Maybe if I'm neither the signified nor the signifier. Maybe if I'm not the pronoun, nor the grammatical agreement of terms. If I am not a form in the noun-class system, an aspect of language, an inherent value in the grammatical category of gender, nor the behavior of associated words. Maybe if I am not a semantic division nor a gender division nor a gender assignment. Maybe if I am not, in some cases, arbitrary based upon my associated noun. Maybe then I can live.

THE UNINVITED

In my office at the university one evening, a male colleague enters and asks if he can ask me a question *real quick* about queer and transness. He mispronounces the *a* in *trans*, as if his throat tried to take the vowel back. He is a mathematician, cisgendered, heteronormative, and has a reputation for wearing culturally appropriative shirts. I answer him that I have just a quick minute because I'm on my way home, needing to catch the bus. I shove folders and papers in my backpack to be sure he understands. He leans toward the open chair.

He tells me he and his wife were having a conversation at church after the weekend's service, and they just honestly don't know what gender is. He says, *like, what is it? how big of a deal is it?*

Following his questions, which wedge between us like a mountain, he sits uninvited in the chair in front of me, half closing the door. I ask him to please open the door.

His questions were likewise uninvited, in fact his presence inside the frame of my office door, which was slightly cracked in the 5 P.M. hour, was not welcome. He persisted through his ignorance, perhaps empowered by the integrity he grants himself on behalf of the church and his family to glean an understanding. His interrogation was neither academic nor scholarly, did not frame itself to benefit the students at our university. He did not ask for resources. He requested a justification of my existence. He wanted to know if my "identity" was real; if I held value.

Uninvited is a word my senses swim in. That *un* followed by *in* is radically oppositional. No matter what follows, it can't be good. *Unintentional*, *unintelligible*, *unintended*, *uninspiring*—adjectives with consequences.

Uninvited is unique: invite, invocate—a reach and appeal to a god beyond human life; creator, archetype. In modern English we no longer *uninvocate*, but we can uninvite.

In my early twenties, Alanis Morissette's song "Uninvited" had a poetic way of stalling me on the word. The song was released in the winter of 1998 and its haunting four-note piano intro on the radio was enough to pull your car over on the road. I was an art student at Kansas State University not quite turning the corner toward being a competent student, painting wildly at home in my notebook while contracting myself to draw on a piece of wadded-up paper in class. The contraction and expansion of being a young artist and a practicing student was perfectly arranged in the D, A-sharp, and G-minor of doom of the piano in the song's chorus. It wasn't sorrow, but a bracing haunt. Alanis's ethereal voice opens with the word *like*, a comparison. *Anyone would be*—a vague, disembodied reference.

The mathematician was not the first individual to mistake my identity for a choice rather than a state of being. Being nonbinary, being trans, these aspects of myself were not part of a multiple-choice quiz. For me, they are inhabited, central to who I have always been, even when I wasn't allowing myself to be aware. The piece that is a choice is the invitation: I may choose to invite you in, or I may not. To my ear, *uninvited* is different than not receiving an invitation. With the invitation, I can choose to offer it or not. If one is uninvited, the choice was never mine. The imposition already occurred.

There is a sovereignty of self at risk in these moments when the persecutor (the privileged mathematician who assumes safety) asserts themselves upon the victim (the trans professor who assumes threat). Philosopher Jill Stauffer coined the term ethical loneliness in 2015 and I wonder to what degree this state of being was at play? Stauffer defines ethical loneliness as "the experience of being abandoned by humanity compounded by the experience of not being heard." She goes on to explain that "for many of us, a deeply embedded story of who we are names us sovereign. We are autonomous selves, capable of consenting—or refusing to consent—to the conditions in which we live. Of course, many of us who tell ourselves that story also know that it leaves out part of the plot, since we didn't get to give birth to ourselves in a world we designed."

A world not designed for us is dangerous, or at least partially so. My white skin armors me with safety—"armors" being a carefully chosen term, as whiteness also weaponizes me. My trans identity, however, is not in the design. My most essential knowing of myself is effectively nonexistent, rendering it as "other" and dangerous in a society built on safety. So is my sovereignty of self, then, no more than a myth when I am relational to others?

"Uninvited" was Alanis's follow-up single after *Jagged Little Pill* swam through the global stomach of pop, rock, and grunge in 1995. What I love about the song is how it comprises just eighty-eight words and how it begs so many questions. Online forums are filled with personal opinions and wildly constructed narratives about the song's meaning. Most of them sound like this: a lonely woman has a crush on a man who loves her but doesn't want to let him in. Never do they suggest that a lonely man is obsessed with a woman and challenges her power until she considers his proposal.

The song was written for the movie *City of Angels* and you can watch the song play along to creepy clips of Nicolas Cage's character obsessing over Meg Ryan's character. He is an angel whose angel-life is missing something; he seems lonely, and he thinks he will find it in her. He chooses to plummet from a skyscraper—a fallen angel—and becomes human, eventually helping Meg Ryan feel more human, too. Then she immediately dies. In a way, they rescue each other from loneliness, yet the moral is that only you can fill your empty spaces.

Alanis also wrote the song from her own experiences, laced with vagueness and mystery. The song is uncharacteristically withheld, so brief it feels like the opening to a horror movie. In a live performance for the Grammys, for which she will earn three awards for "Uninvited," the camera circles around Alanis as she makes pointed eye contact with the audience. She sings lyrics that compare the intrigue one feels for another as uncharted territory, both exciting but unknown. Then, challenging and confrontational, she goes on to directly address the "you" who has assumed they understand something about the love of the song's protagonist. It feels like a potent challenge to a public making her subjective even to herself.

An uninvited person who intends to gain access to you is generally an inconvenience or a threat. The most common noun described by the adjective uninvited is *guest*. Other common phrases are *uninvited memories*, *uninvited thoughts*, and *uninvited comments*. Most paintings with *uninvited* in the title either depict a party with uninvited guests loitering about or are desolate landscapes. Most book covers appear to be dark thrillers or horror. Being uninvited is, simply put, characterized as really bad. A lot of the negativity is rooted in European and colonial culture. There is an insider versus outsider power dynamic at work, as well as an implication of power and privilege. In the case of my colleague, he represented a threat and my nervous system responded by freezing. I am female socialized, and confrontation was not an option in my childhood, so instead of saying *this is not allowed / you're uninvited,* I responded with some basic information while my neck muscles seized. I directed him to the internet and YouTube to get started because, no, sexuality and gender are not the same thing. *Must be strangely exciting / to watch the stoic squirm*, trapping me with his well-meaning and priceless privilege of white, male, Christian, cis, hetero, middle-class intersections.

I see this perceived pattern of victimhood course through my life, listing menstruation and breasts as uninvited, as if my body had been holding me hostage. I list every slight from others that made my body object, that made it more subjective than I had already rendered it. I list, too, the messages I was socialized with: what it means to be a girl, that boys will be boys, that it's best to not respond. In terms of ethical loneliness, to what degree can self-abandonment be seen as the consequence of feeling "abandoned by humanity"?

Returning to Stauffer, it seems I may be in an existential cycle in which I am being returned or forced into an existential solitude. Leaning on fellow phenomenologist Emmanuel Levinas, Stauffer explains the consequence of the existence in relationship to the rumbling background of life designed by others being and having always been. She explains how humans transcend basic existence by becoming grounded as a self in the present moment, only to find this isolation inescapable. It is in the presence of others, through connection, Stauffer states, that we escape solitude. Ethical loneliness, then, is in part *inescapable* solitude—to be refused the liberation offered by others.

I toured the decommissioned prison island Alcatraz when Ai Weiwei's art installations condemned and reimagined the abandoned prison complex. The island, surrounded by saltwater and without fresh lakes or rivers, belongs to the Ohlone and Coast Miwok people yet was subverted by the federal government into a prison for Native peoples beginning in the mid-1850s. The island was first stolen by Spanish colonizers and later European-American colonizers; if you don't believe in ghosts or lingering energy, go to Alcatraz.

Ai Weiwei, who grew up in exile, had to study and imagine Alcatraz from his home in Beijing after his passport was taken when he was kidnapped by the Chinese government in the spring of 2011. He had to embody the isolation of a five-by-nine-foot cell, the precise schedule the prisoners adhered to, the lack of light and touch. Weiwei had to embody another kind of ethical loneliness.

Serving time is a phrase that felt alive in both the abandoned prison and the installations. The two were brought together at times, but always the prison resonated through the art. After exiting the ferry, we were ushered to a ticket line, then into the mess hall—though a twisting concrete staircase spiraled around one side of the looming structure. Inside, Weiwei installed traditional Chinese kites, some in the form of dragons, hanging from the ceiling. Huge and colorful, they seemed to sweep through the decimated rectangle of concrete. Farther in, pointilist prisoner portraits constructed in colorful Legos lay in rows on the ground. You could walk between them like graves, yet the color seemed to bring the faces alive. Walking through the prison, I couldn't help but feel trapped—more than trapped: disoriented, decimated. Rendered and unrendered until I felt gone. In the prison cells, I could see the ventilation hole and imagined the few prisoners who dug the cavity open and found escape. But mostly I imagined loneliness compounded; loneliness beyond full fathom.

There is no transition here that gets us, dear reader, to the end. We are each here: rumbling design around us, under our feet: past, present. It is the future that is unrendered, the future that is worth deliberation.

But there is this: in 1969, an activist group called Indians of All Tribes began a nearly two-year occupation of Alcatraz after it was decommissioned. Kent Blansett describes how, "Akwesasne Mohawk Richard Oakes stood at the San Francisco harbor. From the center of a media frenzy, he offered to purchase the island from the US government. He later swam through the bay's chilling waters to stand on

Alcatraz's shore, claiming 'The Rock' as Indian land in dramatic style."

The occupation, along with many other protests and actions by Native people across the continent involved with and outside of the Red Power Movement, impacted the Indian Termination Act and perhaps most importantly inspired an even stronger future for Native activism.

I haven't told you the reason why I have loved Alanis's song for twenty-five years. After seventy-six words are sung and repeated, Alanis builds to the song's release, singing *I don't think you unworthy / but I need a moment to deliberate.* These words have been woefully misunderstood by listeners more adept at Disney storylines than at listening to the craft surrounding the words. In performance, she translates these vocally and performatively, using pacing and gestures. She is not saying, *you know what, I like you too, maybe we can be together.* She chooses to not dehumanize the person/people being addressed in the song, then places a boundary: to think it over. The sound of her thinking is an epic musical tirade, shimmering cymbals followed by a rock orchestra punching out, unrelenting, haunted, pissed, climactic. I dare any listener to hear the design of boy meets girl in that arrangement. In a 2018 performance of "Uninvited," when Alanis was forty-four years old, she throws her body around the stage during the musical deliberation, spinning, flailing, falling to the stage in exhaustion. Full embodiment shaking off controlling subjectivity of the self.

In the manner of an orchestral rock tirade, I uninvocate any call to any god or any power over me. I address the uninvited with violins and drums slicing away the attachments of other's subjectivities of my body or inner self. The *un* and *in* earn an opposition in response to their confrontation, be that a pause, a no, or a statement making clear the trespass. I cannot change the subjectivity others bring to me, but I can choose how to respond, choose what rides home with me on the bus and who I am in community with along the way.

UNRAVELING VI

In inquiring about loneliness, what I want to know is the nature of love. What I want to know is if love—its essence, emotion, the performance of it—has altered. If the colonial imagination has wrapped itself too tightly around America, squeezing us away from each other. If we can even remember. If we listen to others' ways and reimagine our own ways. Nine years ago, I tilted my ear into extinction, staying in that position for years. I literally drained myself into loss. I wanted to hear that ending, that particular loss. I wasn't working through any struggle with mortality, instead the ultimate mortality for an animal or plant species: *that* last passenger pigeon; *that* last black rhinoceros. Today I lean into the catastrophic loneliness of compounded exclusions: self-exclusion and world exclusion. I want to know if I have capacity—if any of us have the capacity—to stand in our varied realities of the colonial undoing as the stakes of survival intensify and the planet moves on without us.

ORIGIN OF LOVE

December, the last near-moon of the year brightens even the deepest shadows of constellations. We measure these by the depth of our unknowing. I think of constellations as bodies created by distances between spaces in the night sky—not so much the design of stars, but puppet shadows orbiting Earth. In the light of this moon, I am a body bundled in scarf and boots, peering over the edge of the pier. A heron takes a magnificent step toward the shore. I see through her eye a barely perceptible current, a squid with its eight ways of feeling the world. Low tide has revealed the continent's edge before it plummets into Puget Sound where a fire roars somewhere below the ocean's belly.

Late September 2016, a mother named Fatemah in Aleppo gave her daughter a Twitter account. Bana Alabed is seven years old, which means she is learning to read and still believes in sending wishes to stars. Her clothes are printed with snowflakes and Mickey Mouse. See Bana hug her brother. See Bana gaze to the sky from her window sending prayers. See Bana look at the camera as a bomb falls:

Hello, world.
Hear that?

What I want to know is how to stand firmly in the body of a white, colonial narrative; how to be that body, and how to embody love inside the silky gauze of privilege. How to witness dying without corrupting its truth, so when the world's violence is magnified, I can stay awake in its shadow without becoming its shadow. I think this has something to do with locating the knots between my soul and my life, for only a soul untethered in its body can uncover the virulent imagination—can begin to undo the American myth of the white hero. I want to know how to place planets next to gods next to Aleppo's people sharing bread next to my country counting down to its darkest shadow next to my life and discover a love too bright to burn. I want to stand in this fire; this queer body and the most incredible nothing, I want to lean into its molten core.

It is the second decade of the new millennium, and in America, Donald Trump has been elected president. My friend Rae described the morning after the election as a "collective blanket of dread." On the Sunday after, C and I went on a date to the Pacific Science Center in Seattle. We were lured by the idea of being in the presence of something larger than ourselves—dinosaurs, meteors, the way wind shapes geographies of sand. I think we were searching for something to believe in.

On October 1, Bana tweets that the war is like a dinosaur, and hope a past-tense notion.

Lessons in love accumulate through others' origins as we become relational to life outside ourselves. These lessons become reflections that inform us of our self-worth. We can measure our self-worth with a mirror, or by looking into the eyes of another—a judgment that bounces back a portion of our identity. The baby in the womb exists relationally to its mother and learns a lesson about what it means to be in the world: safety, anxiety, love, depression. The baby makes its appearance for the first time and is cradled gently or not (knot); is named a boy or a girl or not (knot); is returned to its mother's breathing or is not (knot). We make our appearances and begin a lifelong relationship to learning how we relate to ourselves and the world.

On October 12, Bana tweets the desire to live without fear.

Q: What are the boundaries of fear?
A: A constellation of silent puppets.

We wandered around the aging science center, gazing at decades-old dinosaur models twisting their necks. When their eyes mechanically fluttered you could squint hard and see a soul in there. C liked the carnivorous dinosaur display the most—imagining a protest against Trump with a bloodied mouth. My favorites were the omnivores, who inhabited a gentle stillness.

On October 3, Bana's mom Fatemah tweets from her account saying they are alive. That they woke up to another morning alive.

After my birth I imagine there was an unbearable stillness (knot). I had rested against my mother's heartbeat my whole life. My mom was one of the last in generations of women electing "twilight sleep" during labor, so I emerged unannounced. Nurses cupped my neck, bathed me. Anonymous ears heard my first cry, saw my first tear. They wrapped me in a pumpkin-colored blanket and showed me to my father. I like to think of these as the tender moments before gender. The nurses didn't need to proclaim me a girl; the word went unpronounced until my father and brother saw me the first time (knot).

On October 16, Bana tweets that she wants to be an author someday.

When I began this essay, I drew a tarot card to keep me from disappearing: #15 The Guardian. In most tarot decks #15 is The Devil. Angeles Arrien describes the Devil as the only card in the deck whose meaning evolves depending upon the mythology being drawn from. In Greek mythology the symbol for the card was half-man, half-goat, to represent sensuality and merriment. In decks drawing from Egyptian mythology the card often features Ra, the sun deity, symbolizing force and energy. Most commonly, the Devil is depicted as evil. Sensuality and evil as an evolution of perspective. A series of tender knots.

#15 The Guardian: not one who is feared, but the human link to wilderness

(1) qualities: fierceness, sexuality
(2) meaning: the real fear is the fear of our own reflection; our inner darkness

I sometimes refer to this as loneliness. What I've been trying to say is inherited loneliness. My father's side of the family is primarily of English ancestry—early colonizers of this land. My mom's family is Iberian, Welsh, German, East African, and Native American, but only "white" has survived in my family's conscious memory.

On October 17, Bana tweets that even the cats are running away from the bombs.

We took our seats in the tiny planetarium, a round room with a control center. Earlier, in the butterfly atrium, orange, red, blue, indigo, and black butterflies navigated human heads and the breaths of excited children. I was happy to be among the living but strangled by the paradox of captivity and the collapsing colonies of butterflies worldwide. Strangled by the relationship between animal and human genocides. Strangled by walking through all the dead bodies.

The science center felt run down by the time we got to the snakes, turtles, and iguanas inside glass cages. We watched children handle the porous arms of starfish and felt ready to leave. Fuck it. Go get dinner. Our love for the world was nothing compared to its pain.

But we stopped at the planetarium. The lights went down to an ochre glow and Joe, the planetarium worker, lit the night sky for us—the sky from my childhood; the one so filled with stars I ran out of wishes.

On October 21, Bana shares a photograph that captures how the war has erased her childhood memories.

See a photograph framing a window collapsed by a bomb. There's a stuffed sheep the color of rubble, a stuffed bear still creased by a child's arm, a flimsy backpack, and an open book with frayed, burnt pages.

I nearly forgot to tell you. There are constellations comprised entirely of darkness. I see them as habitable depths your spirit can travel to when it needs to be alone. Others see a dark river of clouds snaking through the Milky Way, or an emu flying left to right. I imagine its wings opening a great shadow upon the planet. I turn into it; it turns me. I am turned.

On October 25, young Bana tweets that she wants to write about the bombings in her book. That she hopes the world will read her words. That it is her bedtime now.

The origin of my understanding of love might look something like a comfortable room with false floors and hidden panels in the walls. There are secret levers and escape routes, but no maps; plenty of pillows and blankets, but if you fall asleep you may wake up in a reorganized room. I was loved and nurtured, but I'm not entirely sure if my parents had been taught love well enough. As an assimilated "white" American family with long colonial roots on this continent, I'm not sure if their parents had been shown love, or the generation before theirs. In 2002, Mab Segrest, activist and writer, collected five losses of racism: white people's intimacy, affective lives, authenticity, connection to humans and the natural world, and our spiritual selves. In short, the very souls of white people have been compromised for the American dream. Poison and a cure far more poisonous.

Somewhere down a family's lines the nature of love can become a knot made of knots. In the families of white folks, especially here in America, home and ancestors were severed for a promise, or a hope. Each of us is a product of severance, and each of our ancestors' violence our heritage.

Love is an abstraction that lives in our bodies—we can't easily measure it; we feel it—it just is. In my creative writing classes I demonstrate this to my students by saying, *Okay, so let's say tomorrow is show and tell, and I ask each of you to bring in love. What do you bring? Can you bring it to me?* One student will say, *I could bring in a photograph?* Another says, *my dog.*

We quickly realize that love can be represented, but not brought materially forth. I tell them that no matter what I do, when I open my junk drawer at home and rummage through it for love, I'll keep grasping and grasping to the back of the drawer without ever finding it. I think I'm saying that I'll never reach my mother all the way; that I'll never reach past this white inheritance all the way; that love slips in and out of our lives like the ocean's tides.

On October 27, Bana tweets that even the tooth fairy is afraid of the bombings. The tooth fairy has run away and will return after the war ends.

Creation makes the unseen visible; a perception in a moment. It assumes that bringing unlike materials together will create harmony or discord, and that this creation will register in a perceiver's body. Creation can beget action. If I begin with a story from America, place it next to a story from Syria, then maybe our fires will meet. Maybe we will find ourselves in the wing of a constellation.

On November 2, Bana's mother again takes hold of the Twitter account to wonder when they'll see only rain fall from the sky. To see when the bombs over Syria will cease.

As we navigated with Joe through the universe planet by planet, I couldn't help softening into the planetarium's darkness as the sky burned brightly above us. It gave solace to our shared losses; dust clouds snaking over hanging wolf carcasses, ditches of burned bodies. It was as if the sky—as it was revealed to us—gave temporary pause to time. I remembered how the innumerable stars on Massachusetts winter nights lit up the snow. I remembered diamonds and confetti, the sparkles of magic. And though I could recall Mattilda Bernstein Sycamore, a radical trans writer, posting on Facebook that "the opposite of nostalgia is truth," I held nostalgia like a stuffed bear, a temporary cure to a species destroying itself and its home.

Joe zoomed his space navigator toward Venus and described the planet as another rock formation with a molten core, similar to Earth. He said that Venus was the hottest planet in the solar system. Joe asked us, "What does Venus represent in mythology?" Everyone knew the answer; the kids answered first: The Goddess of Love. Staring at Venus I saw the surface was smooth; a pearl or opal; milky. Subtle swirls of warm hues swathed the surface. It was easy to see love in this way: milky, opaque—somehow shrouded.

On November 9, 2016, Bana's mother wonders on her daughter's Twitter feed what will happen to Syrians, and maybe all of us, now that Trump has been elected.

Constellations are created by the fact of boundaries, but aren't boundaries imagined phenomena? And don't facts land against the human heart and become symbols for being alive? A body is no more boundary than an eggshell: it is a perceived creation—an agreed upon orchestration.

For example: Where are the edges of this essay?

The enduring orchestration that some bodies have greater value than others is a created and inherited knot catastrophically affecting people's capacity to love. The most twisted and confused are the most conventional identities: cis-gendered, white, male, able-bodied. The knots of mainstream experience are a strangling; pull the knot and they might strangle you back.

On November 17, Bana implores us to notice what is happening in Syria.

I am trying to stay present with cataclysm. But my privilege is forgetting, or my consciousness is trying to save me from the space between constellations. Will I get lost there? In *A Chorus of Stones*, Susan Griffin wrote: "I do not want to tell you what he found there, or, in setting down the words, to make it a part of my own consciousness." She was trying to show her resistance to writing the reality of the consequence of human violence; the blood tunnels in Dresden—a fire too hot to burn. Griffin later added that boundaries are illusory, that we are all "swept toward the same catastrophe."

Later on November 17, Bana tweets again. She writes that it is not the moon lighting her night sky but falling bombs. She asks for prayers. She tells us she is afraid.

Joe revealed the human heart to me there in the planetarium. He explained the dense system of clouds in Venus's atmosphere. How these dense clouds trap in heat, making Venus the hottest planet, and even drawing a parallel to greenhouse gases and global warming. Then he said, "Look at what happens when our computer looks through the clouds!"

Click! The clouds disappeared and the bloody pulp of Venus's heart thumped before us. A raw mass; volcanic energy: merriment, sexuality, force and energy—it was the true image of the Guardian at the door that became the Devil.

Venus and love and the bloody body for a moment free.

On November 25, Bana clarifies that the smoke in the air over Aleppo is not a cloud. It is their houses on fire or crumbled to dust.

See, the clouds held the heat of the burning heart. The problem is that those who inherit the privilege of safety—those we call "white," cis-gendered, heteronormative—never learned to clear the clouds. That, in fact, the clouds are safety. The clouds have become their love, and, at times, my love, too.

On November 26, Bana begs for someone to save her now.

I've been searching for a new origin story; a way of seeing my own origin and its orientation to love. I am comfortable in between spaces, in the lonely places between the stars playing shadows on Earth's surface. Instead of inhabiting gender, I inhabit the star—so where am I in the boundaries of constellations, in the stories of our human origins? I've been looking for a picture, a body, a representation of a new way of being.

In the song "Origin of Love," adapted from Plato's *Symposium* and written for the trans rock drama *Hedwig and the Angry Inch*, we are shown a time when people still believed Earth was flat. We see a new story of the origins of the human body presented during the age of Greek gods. The song shows that there were three original bodies that looked like rolling kegs: two men sewn up back-to-back, two women similarly stitched, and a man-woman body.

What is crucial in their story is that these people—with four legs and arms, and two heads that could see all around them—didn't know what love was. There was no love. There was no love because this species hadn't yet experienced loss.

Imagine an attachment so secure it is your very being. Imagine that security looking into the eyes of another, recognizing each other's wounds. This is the possibility of emotional activism, a revolution grounded in feeling.

December 16, Bana tweets: *Please* with 10 *e*'s.

Those *e*'s thunk on my head. They are not bombs, but suffering. I lay down symbol after symbol as bodies lie in dusty streets. My art finds us in the puppet theater of hungry ghosts.

Later on December 16, Bana once again entreats her followers to save her from the terror now surrounding her.

A digital countdown webpage started up the day after Trump's election. In thirty-six hours, the clock will run out. My country does not know about bombs, except that they happen to other people in other places. This has become another "new" normal, a silence traveling between history and now, a similar strangulation. My country strangles because it is a country that defined freedom by restricting who had access to it. It is the antecedent we cannot get past because it is the *we* that created white supremacy. And we can barely stand to feel it.

To antecede is to preexist—a time before the time; an origin.

Bana's final tweet on December 16 emphasizes that she needs to be saved *right now*.

Several years ago, it was clear to global communities—as it is clear to me here at my desk a year later—that climactic violence in Syria would take place in Aleppo. Propaganda from worldwide governments and media characterized people in Aleppo differently, and constantly shifted the narrative: Were they insurgents? Rebels? Terrorists?

Vulnerable citizens? They were not given the privilege of between spaces or self-identification.

By the time the Syrian government and Russia's military began bombing hospitals in the summer of 2015, almost five million Syrians were refugees in neighboring countries. The borders to Turkey, the country most positioned to receive those fleeing Aleppo, had been closed. So, when Bana's family gave her a Twitter account it was an attempt to put a human face on the unfolding tragedy. She became the Anne Frank of this unstated world war, except Bana is still alive. Her family was allowed to evacuate Aleppo on December 19, 2016; she arrived in Turkey with over three hundred thousand followers on Twitter.

On December 19, Bana confirms she has escaped East Aleppo.

Bana's survival and the political propaganda following it was a brilliant move in the global chess game of keeping the world quiet. In *This Bridge Called My Back*, Cherríe Moraga wrote that "silence *is* like starvation. Don't be fooled. It's nothing short of that and felt most sharply when one has had a full belly most of her life."

I looked for Venus that night in the muffled constellations of Seattle's city lights. A million lightbulbs burned the beating hearts of the stars. In the museum, I hadn't picked up the butterfly's body, but wish I had. Wish I could have given her a heartbeat, or at least a flutter. So much for the savior. Moraga explained that Audre Lorde asked us all to stare straight into the nightmare. It is here, Lorde explains, you'll find the dream. I have to wonder if white people's nightmares are our constructed lives; if we can see past our gauzy reflections into a beating heart held together by its wounds. Every tweet a stitch over our skin's pucker.

DRAGON

Heat pronounced a fire in my stomach. It spread upward to my diaphragm where a locked box of secrets tried to shield itself. With each inhalation and exhalation my lungs fanned the fire until it rose up my trachea. My throat was a siphon for the flames. I was breathing fire.

Four months earlier I crawled into the darkest part of the shadow. The moon was embalmed in a sheath of red blood, and I pulled it into me like a breath. The autumn equinox had burned the summer harvest, and the rest of us were left to contend with the decaying bodies. I couldn't recognize my own body, or the spirit sunken into it.

I've never kept a diary. My personal thoughts rest somewhere in my body like sleeping dragons. On occasion I make cryptic, symbolic notations of life-altering changes in my monthly planner. The first was an ice cream cone

I drew in 2008 when C and I first had what we call "the great revealing"—sharing life stories, a few secrets. The second and third times were six years later in the summer of fire. I drew a grim face at a meeting at my university when the fragile reality of my trans identity rose to my consciousness. The third was a week later when C returned home from a five-week artist residency in New Hampshire. I wrote "Bad News 1" and "Bad News 2" in my planner. Just before "Bad News 1," on the day C flew home, I had drawn our little house with a fire burning in the chimney, the smoke drifting off to the edges of the world.

The internal inferno moved down to my intestines. When I saw bright blood in my stool I panicked, which only fed the flames. My acupuncturist had never seen heat like this before: as eruption. He said my intestines were so hot that they had to fan open to relieve the heat. When they opened, blood seeped in. We didn't know how to heal it, though I ate so many cold, slimy foods that my face became damp to the touch.

Around the same time, I began coloring dragons. It was winter and I was so tired. I needed to color pictures without humans. Pictures from another time, another world. Pictures that evoked magic. I chose a coloring book illustrated by John Howe, an artist for *The Lord of the Rings*. It was an accordion-style visual narrative that unfolds the story of dragons as written by dragons. The story goes something like this: female dragon gives birth to four new baby dragons who are adorable, mama dragon discovers a castle for them all to live in, baby dragons become powerful adults and summon the spirit of all dragons, dragon family moves into the castle, often sleeping in a room of gold coins (do dragons truly care for wealth?), the dragons write their own history in a book titled *History of Dragons*—a dragon tail wedged into the book's center as a dragon peeks from under the desk. The End.

I heard that when the full bloodred super lunar eclipse occurred the tides around the planet swelled higher than ever before, changing the shapes of maps for the night. I heard that the world might end, that there might be a rise in nervous breakdowns, a rise in violence, and that the divorce rate would increase. I heard about tipping points and tugs-of-war and how dissolution was imminent. I pictured Earth between the moon and sun playing a game with light; the dusty moon becoming a fire in the night sky; becoming a fire.

On the morning of "Bad News 1" we tried to have sex but were strangers. C touched me in a way that wasn't touching *me*—rough and unfamiliar. While they were away, they had started calling me at night from the community dining hall instead of their room. There was a feeling like the edge of the world in their voice, and I tucked the feeling away somewhere in my body. In bed that morning they were lying on the wrong side of me. They had to tell me something. They said they'd met someone in New Hampshire; that they wanted to develop their relationship with him more. I cried from a hidden place inside myself, and the statement registered deep in the muscle tissue of my body. I am pretty sure it is still there—a cinched knot.

The illustration with dragon babies—three still in their eggs—was the only one that interested me. I poured all my love into coloring those eggs; intense patterns of oranges and roses and blues. I saved the cracked open egg cradling a baby dinosaur for last, lavishing it in magenta and black. The eggs nurtured a hope in me—a tenderness for the future that I wasn't able to see in my life, or in the life of the planet. I had been writing a book on the nature of becoming extinct. I leaned over, leaned in, my ear to the ground of that kind of ending. I colored the baby dragon pale blue, softening the tip of the pastel around his floppy wings.

I've always thought of the body as a container being pressed by gravity. The spirit is in there somewhere—maybe crouched down or stretched out. You can stretch it out consciously if you find it and energize it. The spirit drifts from the body, always existing in several realities—especially when we are asleep. My body stores memories that were first detected by my senses (including the sixth), then translated into containers of narrative, then examined for meaning. The container is a place of myths and stories; hidden emotions buried under muscle tissue and deep into bone. My masseuse recently pressed her hands under my diaphragm. "What is that in there?" she said. A graveyard for secrets, I thought.

Sometimes we don't know what our bodies know. Or we know enough pieces of something in a given moment to sort of know, without really knowing. My gender identity rose up from my subconscious like smoke from a flame—not a candle flame or campfire: a forest fire. I stood in a room full of people and suddenly understood how far away from each of them I was. I knew in that moment that I existed, that the eggshell had cracked. I also knew that no one could see me.

As I write this my body feels like a container of tender knots. At the top of my cervical spine—1C my chiropractor says—is a sensitive nexus of vulnerable information. It is a map of my past; each file buried away that I wasn't ready for—my mom's mental illness, my father's absence, the instability of home, not trusting love, not accepting my body, failures, loss. They call this bone Atlas for holding up the world of the head, and mine is in trouble. As I write of C's affair, my crisis with identity and the fire that found me, the knots at my cervical spine tug and pulse. They guard my secrets well.

In Greek mythology, Atlas is depicted on the edge of the world with the dragons. In another story, a dragon named Ladon was instructed by Zeus to guard the three golden apples he treasured. The garden where the apples were kept belonged to Atlas. Ladon and Atlas were trusted companions until Hercules traded the burden of holding up the world for a while in order to get the apples. The deception resulted in Ladon being punished by Zeus—assigned to guard the heavens forever. Many believe that it wasn't the planet that Atlas held, but the universe.

The years prior to "Bad News 1" and "Bad News 2" I had been trying to heal the entire world—to hold it up in some way. I had imagined healing energy emanating from my body and spreading around the planet; a cradle, a container, an egg. I had placed myself inside of species extinction, trying to embody that kind of death. I'd written a book of poetry spells that involved laying the body down on polluted ground and embodying this slow death. In the classroom I was healing lives instead of teaching poetry writing so my students would go on to save the world. I was measuring how much burden I could manage on one axis and our species' violences on the other.

My body had predicted it. Before C's infidelity, I visited them for a few days in New Hampshire. Their artist residency was in a region of New England I think of as home, a shell of memories. I flew into Vermont and rented a car, planning to stay with C in a New Hampshire chalet for a few nights then return to my favorite childhood places. A few days before my flight, my body erupted with a rash. It wrapped around my torso like a twisted Christmas tree. My body was telling me something.

"Bad News 2" day came near the end of the long drought. The ground in western Washington was so parched that I'd come home from a short hike covered in dust instead of mud. The cedar trees were pale, and the human-restored saplings had bronzed under the enduring sun. Wildfires were jumping over streets just outside of Tacoma, and the sunset reflected fire in its horizons. We talked on the couch that night—I hadn't asked them any questions yet: What was the nature of their relationship with him? How far did it go? What had they done, exactly? I noted the position of my body: curled into a ball, neck leaning right, shoulders tightly pinned to my back. I was compressed.

I wrote an email to Rae, a friend and energy practitioner, and said I was breathing fire. Doctors had only prescribed me a little relief: a cooling diet, herbs, and an anti-inflammatory powder for my organs. They talked with me about stress. No one could identify the source of the heat's intensity. Rae gave me the name of a powerful healer in Seattle, so I wrote to him. His response was buoyant. He could journey to my spirit over the weekend, converse with it, and we could work on some healing.

I once heard the story of a dragon who lives at the edge of the world collecting sorrows. I can nearly see sorrow: a grayish cloud, a dirty fog, floating to the edges of what we know. There, a dragon rests forever, collecting sorrow like gold coins in a castle. Does she feed on the sorrow, or dissolve it? Will she hold it for us, so when we return to the edges we also return to our sorrow?

When I arrived in New Hampshire, C gave me an uncomfortable hug. Though they'd only been gone ten days and hadn't begun their affair with X yet, they seemed to be inhabiting another life, one that did not include me. I didn't know why yet, but when C saw me with my shirt off, they looked at my breasts like they were suddenly huge—like they hadn't seen them before. Their look was engulfed. I became a stranger in my body through their reflection. My rash burned in their gaze.

Suddenly realizing that you exist is similar to living in a house with dirty, low-wattage light bulbs, then replacing them with clear ones. Your image in the mirror is somehow a new face, a new body. The spirit staring back has softened its eyes but sharpened its look. You suddenly notice your dusty clothes, the grays and browns you've been clad in. You see the dirty walls around you and feel compelled to wash them immediately. You can't be this dissolving figure framed by walls coated in soot. In fact, you don't want the walls anymore. You only recognize the pile of hair you just dropped onto the floor, and the way you turn your jaw; you recognize that.

C and I were both so panicked that it took us three weeks to have an easy communication between us. By panic, I mean to say that each moment was amplified by each of our deepest fears. You know the feeling: you lose your temper and suddenly you've become your mother; you break a glass and realize that you are a shattered, untrustworthy person. Each of our tiny sufferings struck the chord of our original wounds, until we were a narrative of a single wound re-creating itself over time. They had a lover but that wasn't the crime; it was the intensity of the secret that burned. I was terrified of the earthquake beneath us. I didn't know what would fall, or where we'd be standing when it was over.

On the night of "Bad News 2" we drove to the pier to watch the moon become blood. We were so fragile with each other, tentative. At first the super moon—so close to our air—lit the harbor on the west side of Vashon Island. I glanced at C and saw the moon—a light I've always known in them—illuminate their eyes into a blue knowing. I worried I'd never see that color again, or the tenderness their eyes offer me. I also knew that that worry was amplified, and I wasn't sure which reality would grab hold of me next.

The antumbra crept a halo around the moon, and we were so near to everything: the darkness, the sun, the water, the moon—then a slice of moon took fire.

Astrologers tell us that eclipses force people to deal with their illusions. This is different from fixing something—in fact, it's the opposite: an eclipse shakes and shatters what is comfortable.

As we watched the moon disappear into the darkest shadow, we knew we were watching ourselves, too—dissolving and clarifying. We had no control over the ruddy dark.

I finished coloring the dragons, reserving the final colors for the dragon mama's belly. I imagined all those eggs in there, the ovular tenderness of a shell. I imagined them slipping out one by one, a soundless heat in their nest. I hoped that she liked the colors I chose; that she would respond with love to what I felt was love, too.

At work, when I stopped existing to the world, I wasn't sure if I was Earth colliding with the sun's light, or the moon being drenched in its blood. I knew that I could no longer exist as a woman in the eyes of others, and I knew that I didn't want them to see me as a man either. I was an unbetween: not between those two binaries, but without them. I wanted to feel like a star most days—not a piece of someone else's constellation—but one that burns when the eye is naked enough to see it. Seeing myself this way made gender transition possible—my body told me, and I listened.

C's lover was a trans guy. He had already had top surgery and was on testosterone. He was a fast forward of a body I wanted to be and represented a hollow self-deficit. My body still registers the moment C saw my breasts and looked surprised by their size. Perhaps they were expecting to see X's chest, with its scar lines and smaller nipples. When I think of the moment, hot shame still grabs hold of my neck.

The healer in Seattle, JB, told me that when he visited my spirit it was a sad scene. I sat on driftwood looking out at the Puget Sound while a violent lightning storm raged above. I told him it was my fault; that I was making the storm happen. I told him that I was so tired. When I turned around to look at him, I lifted my shirt and showed him a bloody wound below my rib with a mass attached to it. There was blood everywhere, and I rubbed my hands through it. I hadn't told him that I had been breathing fire.

I learned complicated lessons about love from my family. I was loved and nurtured, but our family lived in a minefield. I learned to freeze on cue. I learned to hide away. I learned that love can come and go like voices inside someone's head. During the season of the dragon, I was learning that love does not hold—it is soluble. It has to be based on change to survive.

A few weeks before I went to the healer I wrote a letter to C. In it I described how, when we first met, we had decided together to make a relationship with an open shape; that we were made of wind. I told them to go where they must, to not erase themselves for me because it would also erase me. I promised to learn to do the same. The letter signified the dissolution of the knots in our relationship; I had finally embodied our realties; I was letting go of what I knew, waiting to see what would form in its place.

I recently watched the DreamWorks film *How to Train Your Dragon 2* twice. It's not a perfect movie, but the dragon named Toothless is incredibly charming, and his relationship with the movie's protagonist reminded me of coloring those eggs. The reason I watched it a second time was for its ending when Toothless stands up against the giant alpha dragon because of his love for his companion.

After being frozen in ice spewed by the alpha, Toothless turns his body blue with heat, and like a starburst, breaks the ice. His entire body illuminates with the blue energy—the fire—of embodiment, and he defeats the alpha.

The alpha is always our own fears. I knew that C and I had co-created our earthquake.

I arrived for my healing appointment and JB bounded from the door of a historical office building in Pioneer Square. In his borrowed office, JB scanned me like an energetic book of knots and light. He read the story my body was telling. He told me that I was being consumed by my wounds—mine, the world's. He said I had my narrative wrong—I had been telling myself the wrong story—it was time to flip the script and embody my body rather than spreading myself out for the world of wounds around me.

Two of his students had also visited my spirit and said these things:

> I was drowning in water that was crystallizing, and the water was my emotions;
> I was digging circular chambers at the bottom of the earth to find light on the other side;
> I was a swan mourning the loss of another swan;
> I had a fire breathing dragon on the bottom of my right rib. The cure for the pain is in the pain. Hug your dragon and let him go.

WOLF TONE

Wolf tone is a dissonance—a tremble within a pattern. Imagine the tiny drums between heartbeats as flutters of air between wingbeats. The tone is a background vibration howling through a song, not so much echo as result. A wolf tone is necessary if we ever hope to hear the planet's turning; if we ever hope to hear it.

Turn left onto Offut Drive, just past the Powder & Keg Grille where the carpet smells like musty beer and mayonnaise, and the mounted deer's eyes see somehow into you—then cross the railroad tracks, through the black iron gate: it's here that cattail moss weighs the conifers into green repose and rain spits in the wind's direction through the watery calls of raven pouring over you, then yips flood into howls opening doors in the forest to times of old growth ecology (that's what we call it)—suddenly a train pulls its chain—a nearer sound, and you are back, rusted and gesturing for the sound that opened time, the sound of what you think is wild—the one that seers your backbone into memory of what it used to mean to be.

To be: *I am here*. The voice inside me is soft, the kind you crane your neck to hear. I once owned a pewter sculpture that listened this way, a violinist tilting their head low to the sound, the strings vibrating against the air's stillness, the wooden echo in the hollow chamber catching and releasing vibrations. There's time here, too—the porosity of sound caused by friction and ease. I lost the sculpture but remember how it taught me to listen. *I am here*; startling, the voice inside the body, its proclamation of existence. But where is it?

The rain stops and I am led through the gates to the wolves; picture a series of round, fenced landscapes, each with a wooden structure inside to act as a den. Lakota, a white wolf scuffed with gray bristles, looks at me for a long time. He raises his large shoulders, bulging the two blades in what looks like playful ambition, and I can see his eyes recognize human more adeptly than the eyes of other wolves I'd seen. To see human in those eyes is to see a cage in a breeding lot; the bed of a dirty pick-up, probably a Chevy or Dodge, probably red or black; to meet the rural Washington breeder making hybrid wolf dogs that sell for $1,000 per pup. For Lakota, human is cage and boundary, human is spoiled meat and hose water.

I feel known in his gaze. Implicit in the way he screws his neck, tilting his ear and eye into me. I feel utterly made in this moment: no gender, no story. To be made in the eyes of an animal is akin to being restored to a natural state: it is a healing, the kind I sometimes run away from because it's the kind that doesn't keep.

Wolf tones occur naturally in stringed instruments: a note's vibration matches the resonating vibration of the instrument's body. Therefore, the tone created is sympathetic—an amplification of a single moment of equanimity; a howl.

Wolf Haven International is a sanctuary for wolves tucked a few miles back from the interstate near Olympia, Washington. The sanctuary houses gray wolves, red wolves, Mexican gray wolves, and even a few coyotes, each rescued from various forms of captivity. Wendy Spencer, director of animal care, describes the time Lakota playfully charged a nervous cameraman—though a sixteen-foot fence was between them, the camera sailed into the bushes while the cameraman sprinted away. It was a wrap. Wendy laughs telling how his imagination really did run away with him, but how this is part of a larger problem. The mythology of the gray wolf versus the reality of this mammal predates the age of reason and stretches its long legs into the twenty-first century—a time when wild is a curated experience, more feeling than reality. *Predates* and *predator*, you hear the distance of the unknown in those *before* moments, the ones before knowing, before understanding, before the bite, before the gun. Wendy admires Lakota's instincts for human fear, an adaptation, perhaps from his former captive life. He gives a few yips, a little howl.

Wendy's blue eyes hold a chill but soften under the gaze of these canines. Her mission is simple: "to let them be—give them food, a companion, space—let them find themselves."

To find oneself. The self tangled in a story is an obstacle to becoming.

As I listen to her, I imagine that she can't build walls high enough for these wolves under the gaze of human stories.

Here, sanctuary is a noun—a person, place, or thing. It has to be given action, a verb, in order to exist in a complete sentence. It must be given a subject, or it must be the subject, so it doesn't become a wolf tone. So it doesn't howl inside a pattern. In the English language all syntactical roads lead to nouns, stacks them like so many pancakes, but offers them very few ways to be. *To be sanctuary.* Close your eyes, listen: what does it mean to be that?

A butterfly darts in a sense. Literally inside a sense. It darts and swerves, fluttering golden symmetries fringed in black. It isn't me, but a story of me, so it is an *other*.

I learn from it. It is small, so I don't fear it.

At the old Vashon Island theater, I see four older white women howl at the piece of visible moon, but this isn't the story. I just watched *Into the Woods*, originally a musical that tells the story of consequences. Four famous Grimms' fairy-tale characters had a wish: to *be* this, to *have* that—to gain some sort of freedom from perceived oppression. There was also a witch, of course, and an evil wolf included in the cast of fairy-tale heroes steeped in longing and hope, making these two the musical's quintessential *others*: those who aren't *us*; those so far on the fringe of what being means that they might as well be aliens from the moon (I'd include "night" as an equal other). The witch, played by Meryl Streep, endures most of the movie under a curse from her mother because she hadn't protected the garden that grew magical beans. At first the garden is portrayed as a magical backyard, but as the movie progresses the garden takes on heavenly symbolism: those magical beans are heaven's apple—the Christian source and consequence of longing—and it was her job to protect them, placing the witch in a nearly holy role.

In the song "Last Midnight," nearly a manifesto, she distinguishes herself as the other, differentiating herself as the witch and everyone else as the world. She places herself outside of normative human culture. The roots of the outsider in recorded human lore extend past the Middle Ages and intersect with stories of evil, benevolent or sexualized werewolves haunting the outskirts of villages; half man, half wolf; man in touch with his animal self and wrought as an outsider because of the connection.

She sings elegiacally with a tinge of rage, stating that she is the hitch no one believes, naming herself the witch. She is the hitch because she challenges everyone's beliefs of what is possible, of what is right, and goes against the majority's decision to protect the boy at the end of the movie.

She is radical. She is what no one believes because she is outside of their constructed realities—a true wolf tone.

A wolf interval is another measurement: a severely dissonant *moment* of tonal frequency. One whose dissonance is so present that it is likened to a wolf howl. This has also been called the wolf fifth. I looked on Wikipedia, and found other subject headings, including "Temperament and the Wolf" and "Taming the Wolf." The writer suggests that the sound must be reduced from the two-dimensional plane to a single dimension. They go on to state, "The wolf can be tamed by adopting equal temperament."

Near the movie's end, the witch is swallowed by the earth. She calls upon her mother—and here we infer a holy mother or mother earth—to come for her, make her hunched and ugly again. She is done with the human world. Just before the earth swallows her, she places a final curse upon humanity: you are alone now, you tend the garden, separate and alone.

She abandons them to suffer alone, in dominion over the planet, forever disconnected, down on all fours trying to remember what it really means to be.

A *refuge* is inherently solitary and appeared in church literature in the early twelfth century as the Latin *refugium*, meaning "God's house" or even serving as an epithet for God. The term *sanctuary* came later, beginning also as a house for God, then for humans to feel God, then as evasion from evil. Finally, it was used to mean a way out.

I once moved from Seattle to an island off the coast of Washington. I think I used it as a way out, though I'd like to say it was a sanctuary. I like the comfort of sanctuary, how it seeks, how it is a refuge that is available and offered. But that stinks of illusion: that the land is there waiting to house me. That I will find something there. I left the dense urban noise of Seattle because my nerves were on fire, my senses charred. Vashon Island offered a reprieve, a more natural state of living. I am grateful for this. I am learning the land's rhythm again, but I must admit that it was a way out; a way out to find a way in. Another objective use of place. The day I ran into a statue honoring early colonizers was the day I ran into a reflection of myself.

And as a trans person—one who doesn't inhabit gender—I am *other* here—rendered as "outside" of the usual narrative of the island that boasts a liberalism clouded by privilege. The local coffee roaster has an annual event in which they light up a hundred pumpkins to celebrate Halloween. There are the evil smiles and spiky eyebrows, crooked lids, and cats carved from homogeneous patterns. But that night all I could see were luminous eyes upon me—a nongendered creature in the discomfort of another culture's sanctuary. That night, I was the witch, and they the world.

What does it mean to be "other"? What am I referring to if I say that there is an *other* under there? In 2015, ten Black people were killed by white supremacist Dylann Roof inside a sanctuary—a mostly Black church in South Carolina. They were the other, and in the United States they have always been the other. The not *us*; the *us* defining refuges. Jelani Cobb explains, "For Black Christians, the word *sanctuary* [in the late sixteenth century] had a second set of implications. The spiritual aims of worship were paired with the distinctly secular necessity of a place in which not just common faith but common humanity could be taken for granted." In this sense, then, sanctuary was a way not to be *other* in the face of white supremacy.

Placing this event next to the occupation of the Malheur Refuge in Oregon, we see the glaring cultural disparity around the notion of a sanctuary. The Bundy militia is part of the group who define refuges, and they want to change the definition. Through the use of arms and an incredible sense of privilege they intend to take back public land—land that never belonged to colonizers in the first place.

The history of land in colonized America is a drawer that, when opened, is filled with millions of secrets wrapped in terms like "manifest destiny" and "settling." All the hungry ghosts of colonizers come screaming out, swallowing witches and wolves, rolling in the dense fog of forgetting and silence. But look carefully—the drawer is one compartment of a card catalog enunciating the history of this land; a true etymology in tribal languages and traditions inherent to wind and water and animal and spirit. A fabric of African song and language and sacredness still coursing a tenderness in America's soil.

As a trans person and poet I seek the *other*. The one buried under each of our stories. The one that wants to simply be; to have what Wendy described for the wolves, in which one has enough food, companionship, and space to simply find oneself. The tension here, then—the howling chord in the human pattern—is in the universalization of meanings. That we might skip the necessary cultural landscapes of a sanctuary in order to seek refuge in the universal because of a whitewashed perspective. The tension is that sanctuaries are human notions that are far more diverse than the notions of the ones who have written the commonly available books and dictionaries, therefore the audience for language makers—for most nature writers—is not universal, but white and normative.

We need wolf tones—the discordant howls in the pattern—to creation friction. How else will we discover the ease without friction, without disturbance?

Here's a wolf tone: an allowance to myself; to exist in constant emotion—a state of grief or love instead of hope. It is this very grief that keeps me going, that connects me to love, that may align us. The grief is personal, it shapes my spirit, keeps it connected. I keep writing and teaching and loving because I am so far inside the loss that the losses become the very shape of myself.

Others use hope. In fact, hope is marketed as the primary response to grief. But if you know Jack Gilbert's poem, "Michiko Dead," then you remember that grief is a box we carry. We never put it down. We learn to live with it. Hope, on the other hand, is a Western construction. It is an ideal to live by. An ideal that keeps our hands clean and our minds bright with illusion. It is a metaphor that we see in the earth, a metaphor that keeps us going in the face of maddening destruction. It is a magical bean. But it is not the moment. The moment is our beings in this place now: spirit, reason, emotion—the interconnected, erotic, living texts handed to us by Audre Lorde, Cherríe Moraga, Gloria Anzaldúa. These words, your breathing mingling with the room's air. This is the moment. Hope is the future—the hope for things to become better; to become—not to be.

As I leave Lakota and Wolf Haven, do I hope for the wolf in its sanctuary? The wolf in Yellowstone? I remember when

I drove away from Yellowstone's gates the animals disappeared instantly. Now you see them—bison, pronghorn, elk, mountain goat, coyote, wolf, eagle, beaver—now you don't. Eight hundred miles home, they never returned. It already happened. The regulation, the loss, the colonized imagination of sanctuary—a version of extinction—already happened.

I choose to carry love and grief for the living world around me, whether it's the rust-spotted pear tree leaning onto my balcony or the single salmon leaping its green-silver fin up the glacial river. I choose connection in the reality of regulated lands, loving those boundaries until they dissolve into open-ended inquiry. I choose to feel the vibration before the sound, then I make its meaning. This is my wilderness and my survival. This is my wolf.

UNRAVELING VII

There's a moment when summer switches direction, turns away. I feel it in the energy of trees, this subtle shift before equinox. Since April it's been sugar, energy, flower, pollen, fruit, but on this day in September in Tacoma, the city I now live in separated from C, you can feel the body's sugar—its sweetness, oils, and energy—change circuit, transcirculate its current inward. It's not a click, nor a flick of a switch, but feels like one. It's a collective whisper: we've peaked, now retreat.

Now retreat, it's collective—a great inward turn—though we experience it body to body. Sharper edges to the air, crisp ends of leaves, the skin on my forehead suddenly flaky. It's like we all can't shed fast enough. I wonder how collapsing civilizations before ours have experienced this, the slow dissolution after a collective peak, or the swift interruption of collective life from colonizing violence and disease or severe drought. The passenger pigeon's population was so thick the sky turned red from a passing flock. It took only a handful of years to destroy their species. The extirpation of megafauna, the marginalization of the gray wolf, the massacre of buffalo—all collapsing civilizations in North America. What of global collapse, the great turn inward of planetary circuits?

Planetary circuits are built on change, are spirit-like. The late season spirit is internal and down, and a moth suffers in my porch light. Its breath seems to heave, the lower portion of its body shedding away somehow. All summer I partnered with my black cat, Cielo, to hunt moths. It's her nightly hunt—her hearing so attuned I swear she can sense a moth before it's there. She is the hunter. My role is to hold her up to the lamp once each night, let her paw at a few bugs until they fly away. It's that moment of predator partnership that matters to her. Sometimes I swipe a moth from the ceiling with a broom. Tonight, she swipes at the suffering moth on her own, kills it too easily. I toss its body into a spiderweb near the lamp. The spider glides down a silk string, spins circles around the carcass, creates a moth mummy in seconds.

In seconds, my breath changes everything about who I am. I tried to find wholeness while summer was in increase. Some sort of well-stitched container for my body; a spirit settled with grace. So much of my life has been spent in a body bisected: my waistline a gaping equator between two halves of a divided planet. I'd been on T for two years and felt a male-developed top half and stagnant, estrogen-stubborn lower half. The loneliness of living inside others' views of my body and gender were and sometimes still are a space inside me that floods and swallows.

Floods and swallows, the gaping throat of words. If there is a grammar to embodiment, I can't write it. My words, all sutures and sew. Embodiment is rare, takes me, surprises. When I enter into the chatter of a tree's canopy talking through wind; when I feel seen and actualized by a loved one or the gaze of a crush that says *I see you*; when a poem sends me into what feels like the weightless space of the universe, I know I am whole. I love semicolon and em dash and look there for a hinge. Syntax is fashion, anaphora a pulse. I fracture and bridge; divide and marry—there's no end to this reimagination. But in the end, it's all body and only body. It's only body, I say—this life and every life before.

This life and every life before, the overwhelm is located somewhere between the universe's edge and your body. It is easiest to think of it as an ocean wave—sometimes subtle as it draws the ground from under your feet, other times slamming you with planetary surge. It is made from these two elements: push and pull. Each is fire staying alive in the sea, neither lingers on its effects. The overwhelm sounds like a muffled heartbeat laced with a large animal's warning moan. It is sheath and rope, cave and grave, it does not constitute with endings; it does not have a constitution.

A constitution has a linguistic heart, *together with*. In a body *together with*, we place felt-sense over what our body remembers to blend with the pain. In a relationship *together with*, we hold to boundaries that make space for us to love, facing wound to wound. In a neighborhood *together with*, we extend care to everyone whenever it is needed. In workplace *together with*, we find shared purpose beyond the capitalist dogma of individual success and consumer product. In town *together with*, we remember our histories and build a fair future for every person and family. In country *together with*, we are responsible to our country's history and work to repair harm by creating new systems to grow into. In global *together with*, we see through the economic and social systems co-creating a scale of value for people and view the planet as an ecological and storied homeland irreproducible and alive without us.

Without us is full fathom, just as with us is full fathom. This summer, I swam in lakes, feeling the depth of my body register whole: a circuit, a unit. The lakes did not measure me. Water displaced around my body, tiny schools of fish shifted direction. I was in, then I was out. That is all.

Is all life measured by what is known, or does the imagination include a life?

A life is a web interconnected by all it touches. I am trying to wind and unwind silk when I tell you my story. We were sitting on the tile floor, the tiles warmed by the fireplace. I wanted to be a fire—to succumb and rage, but mostly I listed the shapes that made me into one who sometimes feels like smoke drifting to an everywhere that neither holds nor releases. The spiderweb was the woven architecture for a moment. It was my story, for a moment.

For a moment, I need you to know that every wisdom occurred before we arrived; that every statue is a monument to our unique existences and we falter at the statue's base because we can't see its whole form. So maybe if we shrink it down. Maybe if I am the fire and the smoke,

I might find my raw nature—something like the moment before death, or the baby passed over the dying in a blessing of love.

Love shifted for me in 2020—not what it means but what I allowed it to do. In the collective inward shift of global quarantine and mass uncertainty, I moved inward toward myself. In therapy one day I said *I think I deserve to be my full self.* I may have meant my own full fathom. In the old days, a fathom was a length measured by pressing your fingertips together. Stretch your arms forward to measure fathom. What is the measure of outstretched arms? What can you imagine holding in that expanse?

Expanse can be measured by imagination or specific measuring systems. One requires sense, the other a method based upon other systems, many of them planetary. The unknown is a poetic expanse, one often regulated by fear. In *The Body Is Not an Apology*, Sonya Renee Taylor clarifies that "to be fear-facing is to learn the distinction between fear and danger. It is to look directly at the source of the fear and assess if we are truly in peril or if we are simply afraid of the unknown." As I look at the expanse of this present moment, I face nothing that I know and everything I hope will be. My measuring stick is based upon change, my response adaptive. There's a hyper-modern element of survival at play as social and economic systems collapse and as the environment responds to human extremism. It is a structural unraveling.

Unraveling a knot has two parts: unweaver and thread. The unweaver can be a spider, wind, human, idea—any force to unsnarl two ends of one body. The unknot is the unimposed agreement of the body or bodies, where they once intersected and bound: lump, mound, clump—all according to the weaver's design. The unknot is an unbetween, a place of liberation.

A place of liberation is not a place without pain; it is more like measuring every emotion all at once in your outstretched arms. When C and I could no longer manage the growing measurements between us, we learned how to separate. The separation was *together with*—together but with the boundaries we each needed to self-determine the shape of our individual selves. We went to couples therapy and learned that, for us, to truly be there for each other, we had to let each other go. The night before my moving truck was in the driveway, it took a Pangaea-splitting cry in my body to make space for the change. I was pulling apart my body to make space for what would become.

What would become is a process of transanything, anything becoming, or water becoming vapor becoming us. It's a finding of myself within myself and within narratives larger than me. A lean into expansiveness, the full fathom of measureless existence. In this space, I can shoulder the losses, swim in a lake that doesn't need to discover me. I can come up for air, wind gulping the language of a nature of me and beyond me.

SHE USED TO BE MINE: AN AFTERWORD

Here is one last way to lose our way.

My fingers rub over the stone until I find memory. The memory is a feeling, a kind of love between us. The stone shows me how the river spills down the mountain like grief, the lazy runnels around fallen trees and precipitous arches down sheer cliffs. It tells of ice floes at the top, crystals of ice a cathedral window floating in occasional sheets. There's the story of the glacial moraine dropped along the riverbed, the stone breaking away, a piece of time tumbling to this riverbank. I experience this history—the stone pressed gently in my palm; my spirit open to the pulse of energy of this being. My animacy mingling with the stone's, we experience each other. We are living texts.

Twice I've been told to grieve the girl inside me. Burial, funeral, ritual—three words blend into one; atmospheric conditions of rhyme, or connotative erasure. Say them aloud and feel your throat vibrate on the first syllable, *bu, fu, ri,* then how air from your lungs presses your tongue down into *urial, uneral, tual.* Each a tiny echo landing in small endings inside your mouth.

I struggle to wrestle America from my mouth and find a habitable language. *Queer* squeezes from its source of syllables but I want to live inside the word like a delicate pocket. Robin Kimmerer wrote "a *bay* is a noun only if water is dead," and sometimes I feel unalive in the word, in the world, like it must be surrounded by a dozen metaphors of stars to find enough space. Or how most days I am the only one in the room seeing the rift in our realities of existence; how I am *here*, but never quite *there*. In *Braiding Sweetgrass*, Kimmerer goes on to write, when *bay* is a noun, it is defined by humans, trapped between its shores and contained by the word.

In my poetry class, a young woman from Palestine shares her struggle to blend her mother language, Arabic, with English. She has written a poem that is liberatory, dismantling and refusing others' perceptions of her. She shares this with the class in English on the one hundred and tenth day of Israel's genocidal siege upon Palestine. She does not place words on this. She does not place words when I ask her how she is. She does not attempt to contain this with words.

In my earbuds, Sara Bareilles sings about the lostness of not recognizing oneself. In her song, "She Used to Be Mine," her voice begins fatigued and hollow, unmakes my body. I am pinned to the moment of her tone. The moment is without time, floating but somewhere right here. I look down the line of my body, so mine, yet so utterly unrecognizable. Why is it so easy to memorize the body of another, but feel so profoundly lost for your own? Is this what Bareilles means when she describes how others take more than they give? Have perceptions so erased me from myself?

I was relieved to dismantle her: the breasts, one larger than the other, the breasts strapped against the body, the rounded hips and butt like an automated cat-call generator, the monthly blood, light for a day, heavy for another, then slowly drying up. Not the personal *my* but the objective *the*. The *she* I never wanted.

Two years after C and I dissolve our relationship I meet a queer woman who my friends hope will become my lover. On the drive to the restaurant to meet her I almost share my dead name with my friends, but one interrupts and says, *We are your friends who don't know this. You get to have us not know this.*

Years before I lay on a thin pallet at the Hothouse cooling off. The Korean-style bathhouse is located under Seattle's oldest lesbian bar, the Wildrose. I rarely felt lesbian enough to have a drink at the bar, though I knew it was a place for queers and inclusive of all women. Walking by at night I'd find myself looking at my reflection in the windows instead of looking inside, not particularly here nor there in that moment. Later, from the soaking tub below, I can just make out the thump of shoes dancing inside lesbian-enough bodies. I shift to a tiny floor pallet to cool off and am charged like sudden lightning: I am not living. I am a self of yous inside a skin-sewn body and slowly dying.

And a memory from a decade before: I stand at what would have been the door to my family's home on Poplar Street. Economy and time have demolished the structure, but I can feel my mom's sadness and warmth in the carpet of wildflowers healing the earth.

Dispossession as scattering, as exodus; as the expulsion from land, possessions, home, self. Or to be mislaid, as in sacrificed. The mislaying of a people. The expulsion of self. While I complete final revisions on this book rooted in undoing the knots of history, mothers in Gaza carry their breathless infants in white sheets, stitches weave in and out of stretched abdominal skin without anesthetic, and babies weep for parents and homes they do not have. To watch genocide livestream is to redefine the sutures of possible knowing; it is neither here nor there, but in the measureless unknown of our capacity to witness and Palestinians' capacity to survive. It is the needle and thread of colonial structures weaving an old pattern—a future created by violence.

Neither here nor there might be a transanything, but it shouldn't take dying to achieve it. It is found in the sovereignty of one's body, one's story. It rests in the palm of one's self determination, unencumbered by cruelty but somehow blooming forth from it. There are the lessons of death carried within it, but it is hearty with possibility.

Kimmerer returns to the Potawatomi language and suggests a shift in language from nouns to verbs, from naming to being. She writes, "to *be* a bay—releases the water from bondage and lets it live." She finds wonder in the positionality of *to be*, suggesting the community of live intersections coursing interconnectivity between and through each other. If each word is alive. If each word curates original aliveness within you. If we witness and survive each other's suffering, will we learn to let each other live outside of bondage? Kimmerer states, "all are possible verbs in a world where everything is alive."

The stone in my palm is cool. All the changes that ever occurred to create this temperature have already happened. Then I plucked it from its narrative, laying my pulse into its story until I could hear it—co-creating this moment with my heat and the stone's river temperature. The stone is grace because its spirit and my spirit are mirrors for each other: we see our forms through each other.

To queer is to create; it is generative; it is transanything. My body has a male appearing chest, my neck thick and sturdy. I am called bro and sir. My vagina is still there, but with a new vibration. Everything I am is what I was, but not quite *there*. I am found in this loss.

In this loss, too, is the co-creation of one version of a life C and I wrote together. There's the story, and there's the way the story turns to find new ways of being. C and I are family now, still there, but another new vibration.

The mountain's beauty does not come from the fact of being seen, but from being illuminated by the earth's secret depths: by the living narrative of stone and bone and sky in the earth's core. The very depth of change is what shows us the mountain, reminding us of its story as a living text. By seeing it you have joined its story, not defined it.

There is a hum to genocide. It is in our bodies. There is a hum to animal and plant extinction, a gentle wave in the rocking of geologic time that is cradling our bodies. In this epoch defined by human activity, new scales of grief are needed. Holding together. Holding back. Caring for and nourishing. I will always be the little kid at the window of a demolished home looking among wild red clover for the scent of my mom's hair, acknowledging the privilege of this reflection, the retreat and expanse of my questions as we enter a future of uncertainty, though how could it be any other way.

ACKNOWLEDGMENTS

The author would like to thank the editors of the following publications, in which these essays first appeared:

About Place Journal	"Restoration of Wolves"
Bellingham Review	"Lonely Species"
Creative Colloquy	"On Senses: A Nature Essay"
In Layman's Terms	"Paperclip: A Story of Invasive Species"
Kenyon Review	"Transanything"
Moss	"Snap the Whip"
Tupelo Quarterly	"Wolf Tone"

The words in *Transanything* were found and strung together across many Indigenous lands in Turtle Island and I am deeply appreciative to all the tribes who care for these lands, their memories and wisdom, especially the Puyallup Tribe and all Coast Salish Tribes for stewarding the lands where this book grew its deepest roots.

I am indebted to too many scholars, theorists, artists and activists to name, but will highlight June Jordan, Audre Lorde, Claudia Rankine, Joy Harjo, Joshua Whitehead, Nell Irvin Painter, Mab Segrest, Prentiss Hemphill, Mattilda Bernstein Sycamore, David Wajnarowicz, Brenda Hillman, Jorie Graham, Lena Khalaf Tuffaha. and Rainer Maria Rilke as guiding lights throughout the development of my thinking for this book to become what it is.

To the Famous Wolf of Yellowstone, 832-F, my co-protagonist, thank you for finding me. So much of this book is dedicated to you.

Thank you to my therapists, B and Rain.

To the singers and songwriters on repeat over the many years of this book's writing—Whitney Houston, Brandi Carlile, Alanis Morissette, Patty Griffin—your voices have measured time for me.

Thank you to many colleagues at the University of Washington Tacoma for years of support and to the students who ignite my curiosity and heart.

Thank you to Lois, Laurin, Rae, Erin, Fern, Ashley, Roderick, Danielle, Danica, and my Tacoma crew. An extraordinary note of gratitude to Sarah A. Chavez for being my poetry and teaching partner-in-crime.

To my parents and brother, an immeasurable thank you.

To Corinne Manning, thank you for trusting me with our story. This book is a partial map of our journey, and I am proud to call us family.